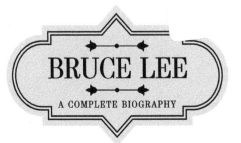

BRUCE LEE

A COMPLETE BIOGRAPHY

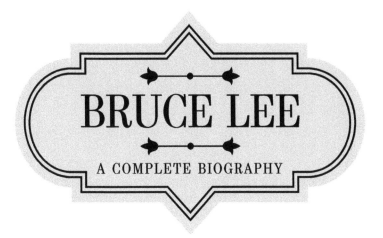

BRUCE LEE

A COMPLETE BIOGRAPHY

ABHISHEK KUMAR

PRABHAT
PRAKASHAN

Published by
PRABHAT PRAKASHAN
4/19 Asaf Ali Road,
New Delhi-110 002 (INDIA)
e-mail: prabhatbooks@gmail.com

ISBN 978-93-5521-492-8
BRUCE LEE: A COMPLETE BIOGRAPHY
by Abhishek Kumar

© Reserved

Edition
First, 2023

Price

Printed at

Author's Note

On July 20, 1973, Hollywood lost its highest paid actor, Hong Kong lost its national hero, and the world lost the most influential martial artist of all time. Bruce Lee, son of Cantonese opera star Lee Hoi-Chuen, was one of the biggest names in Hollywood at the time of his death. He is credited with introducing the East to the silver screens of the West. Lee's premature death at the age of thirty-two brought shock waves across newspapers and television channels all throughout the world. In one of the TV interviews given to Hong Kong radio after his death, his widow Linda recalled, "It seems we were always beginning on a new life—beginning in films was a new life for us. Becoming famous and breaking records—everything was new all the time, and he kept saying, 'This is just the beginning'."

His greatest passion in life was Kung Fu—an ancient Chinese martial art unknown in the West until 1965, the year he made his first television appearance. A Kung Fu master, an actor, and a philosopher, Bruce Lee embodied the idea of a complete human being—one with a strong body and a critical mind. He studied a system of Chinese Kung Fu for nine years called Wing Chun and is considered one of the art's most talented and articulate exponents of this art. His teacher in this art was an elderly Hong Kong Chinese master by the name of Yip Man.

Apart from having a keen interest in martial arts, Lee nurtured a very distinguished taste in philosophy and literature too. He was an ardent reader of *Confucius*. He tried to incorporate Confucian philosophy and teachings in his life. Bruce Lee's interest in philosophy, distinct from the Western ethos as the love of knowledge, was a passion that remained with him throughout his life. He taught Americans about Chinese philosophy and culture for six years. He lectured in the Pacific Northwest about the delicacies of Chinese thoughts. In an interview given to Pierre Berton on December 9, 1971, he said, "Do you know how I want to think of myself? As a human being, because I mean, I don't want to sound like, you know, as Confucius say, but under the sky, under the heaven, man, there is not but one family. It just so happens, man, that people are different." Many considered Bruce Lee, an individualist as he always put the individual at the center of all his philosophies and believed in the idea of self-introspection to understand the real "us."

Lee's life was one riddled with fights. During his childhood, he fought against recurring illness, weak physique, and absence of guidance. Later in life, he fought against an uncertain and an unstable career in martial arts. The uncertainty made him to toy with the idea of becoming a professional dancer. He even went on to win Hong Kong's Cha-Cha championship. But, it was Kung Fu, which he had practised all his life that brought him the tranquillity he craved for.

At the age of nineteen, he moved to America. The first thing he did after moving to the United States was to join a school, and in no time, he learnt to write and speak English better than many native speakers. A few years later, he opened a Kung Fu school and began making a living by teaching Americans the art of the Shaolin. He questioned the traditional styles in his teachings. Both the American and Chinese martial art societies resented his heterodoxy. For such a young man to stand up against thousands of years of tradition and esteemed power was considered a direct threat to the status quo.

Bruce was known among his friends for his short-temperedness and his competitive attitude in life. He wanted to be the best in whatever he did. Such an approach, for obvious reasons, won him more adversaries than his friends. At first, it was then Hollywood star Steve McQueen whom Bruce Lee vowed to beat, and then it was James Coburn whose name he added to the list of his competitors. However, notwithstanding a long list of rivals, his toughest struggle was with himself.

He detested mediocrity and always pushed his limits, both physically and mentally. This often resulted in abrupt mood swings. He also complained of having nightmares. Whether it was his hate for mediocrity or his fear of it that made him a soul so difficult to comprehend, one can't say.

His tenacity can be understood from the fact that only a year after being rejected for an acting part, he went on to become the highest paid actor in Hollywood. His journey from rejection to recognition was fraught with many obstacles. At first, he suffered a back injury, which rendered him crippled for months. It was one of the most frightening periods of his life. Nevertheless, exhibiting intense dedication and willpower, he soon moved out of this period and continued on his path to international fame.

In 1973, the year of his death, he was at the zenith of his career. His movie, The Chinese Connection, had won the Special Jury Award at the 1972 Oscars. With this win, he had already shut his critics. After having conquered all the frontiers, it was the time for him to slow down and take some rest. But, Lee had other plans. He continued to work harder and kept pushing his boundaries.

In his quest to achieve greatness, he often ended up isolating his soul from the scrutiny of the world. "An open book" wasn't a phrase, one would associate with him. It seemed as if he was seeking solace in solitude. He didn't boast of a long list of people whom he would call "friends" but though short the list might have been, he made sure that he keeps it close all through his life.

"A victim of impulse" is how many of his close friends recall him. On the contrary, to what the characters he played on the screen portrayed, Bruce could never find placidity in Kung Fu. It was always around him, but never with him. The toughest task for him, both on screen and off-screen, was to discipline himself. And the biggest hurdle for him was his short- temperedness and the other being his overconfidence.

Through his work, he had inspired generations of youngsters all over the world and continued to do so even today. His posters adorn the walls of the rooms of the teenagers across the globe who see in him a fighter, a teacher, and a role model. Many stories have been woven around his death. But instead of analysing his death, one must learn from his life. A life, short yet large, elated yet dejected, and singular yet banal. It is a lesson brimming with wisdom and philosophy for a reader to enrich his/her life in its every facet. This is a story worthy of being told and read thousand times.

– **Abhishek Kumar**

Contents

The Story Begins

L ee Hoi-Chuen was an actor with Hong Kong's Cantonese Opera. Primarily known for his comic roles in the theatre, he could often be found smoking opium in Hong Kong's suburbs. He would also frequent the gambling events in the neighbourhood. He considered himself more of a singer than an actor, but his fans begged to differ. They enjoyed his flamboyant gestures and knife like emotions on the stage more than him singing in the high-pitched vocals. His roles brought him immense name and fame, and within years of starting his career as an actor, he soon owned several apartments throughout the city.

Among the multitude of his fans, one was special. Her name was Grace. Raised by a Chinese mother and a German father, she embodied the values and cultures of both the East and West. It was at the age of nineteen that her family moved from Shanghai to Hong Kong. She often accompanied her father to the opera concerts of Lee Hoi-Chuen. In no time, she fell in love with the most successful opera singer in Hong Kong. She was a regular at his events and used to make sure that she sat close enough to the stage for Lee to notice her. Her efforts bore fruit, and the two soon got married and moved to an uptown apartment situated at Nathan Road in Hong Kong.

Their efforts of starting a family suffered a huge setback when their first child died weeks within birth. The death was followed by a period of immense mental and emotional torture for the couple. The episode left them vulnerable enough to fall into the trap of superstitions. The superstitions demanded the second child to be a girl; the two decided to name their forthcoming child Phoebe to confuse the bad spirits. Months passed, and the couple was blessed with the birth of a boy whom they named Peter.

During their visit to the United States as a part of Lee's opera concert, Grace realised that another child was on its way. On November 27, 1940 (the year of dragon according to the Chinese zodiac) at some time between 6 and 8 A.M. she gave birth to the third of their five children. It was a boy, and like the previous time, to confuse the spirits, the couple gave it him a girl's name, Sai Fon. They even went on to the extent of piercing one of its ears. They later named the child Jun Fan, but it was the nickname Bruce, given to him by the supervising physician that stuck with him for the rest of his life. Bruce later in life went on to change his last name to Lee from Li.

❑

Hong Kong

Walking by the Avenue of Stars located by the waterfront at Tsim Sha Tsui, Hong Kong, one is greeted by a 2.5 meter bronze statue of Bruce Lee in his classic "ready to strike" pose, as seen in the 1972 movie Fist of Fury. For Hong Kong, Bruce Lee was more than a movie star. He was its national hero, its ambassador, and its son. It was through his movies that the Hong Kong film industry scaled new heights in the world of motion pictures. It was through his movies that the world was introduced to the culture of the country. It was through his movies that Hong Kong made its mark on the map of the world as a modern nation.

Hong Kong, or The Fragrant Harbour in Chinese, or as officially called, the Hong Kong Special Administrative Region (SAR) of the People's Republic of China, is an independent terrain on the Pearl River Delta in East Asia. On its west is situated the territory of Macau, whereas the Chinese province of Guangdong boundaries it to the north. With a total land mass of 1,106 square kilometers and over 7.3 million inhabitants of various nationalities, it positions itself as the world's fourth most densely populated autonomous state or territory.

After the First Opium War of 1839, Hong Kong became a British settlement with the eternal cession of the Hong Kong Island, charted by the Kowloon Peninsula in 1860. It was later followed by a 99-year lease of the New Territories signed between the British and the Hong Kong administrations from 1898. Hong Kong was then captured by Japan during World War II until the allied forces reconquered it in 1945. In the early 1980s, talks between the United Kingdom and China give rise to the 1984 Sino-British Joint Declaration. The declaration paved the way for the handover of the dominion of Hong Kong in 1997 when it became a special administrative region (SAR) with a high degree of autonomy under the People's Republic of China.

In the 1970s, the country undertook several reforms that shaped its future. For the most of the decade, it was under the leadership of its longest-serving and reform-minded Governor, Murray MacLehose. He reformed every facet of the country's economy. It reinvented itself from a manufacturing hub into a financial center. The market also began leaning towards businesses and franchises.

During this period, the country's culture also underwent major changes. It developed a fusion of western ideas and eastern values. It not only kept many Chinese traditions but also experienced a baptism of western culture.

But, before the reforms of the 1970s, the country was plagued by grinding poverty, and it was during those days that Bruce Lee was growing up as a boy in the filthy streets of Hong Kong. The Hong Kong of his childhood was choked with crowded markets, narrow streets, lorries, taxies, pushcarts, neon signs and other paraphernalia of the era. While one corner of the city smelled of exotic dishes, the other reeked of sludge.

Bruce Lee spent most of his childhood days fighting, hiding, playing, and amusing himself in the narrow, dark, and filthy streets of Hong Kong.

❏

Early Days of Bruce

Few months after his birth, Bruce Lee's parents returned to Hong Kong from America. The sudden change in climatic conditions took baby Bruce Lee by surprise. He had problems adjusting to the humid weather conditions in his country. Soon he fell ill and hence began his perpetual state of illness. A long period of illness made certain that he remained underweight throughout his childhood.

Bruce Lee lived with his family in a spacious apartment on Nathan road, but he could not enjoy the luxury of the space for long. When his uncle, his father's younger brother, died, Bruce's father took it upon himself to look after his brother's family. This led to a situation where about 20 members shared that apartment, often accompanied by animals such as hens, dogs, cats, etc. Among all the members of the family, his favourite was an Alsatian dog named Bobby who often slept with him in his bed.

It would not be right to consider that Bruce Lee came from an unprivileged background. As mentioned earlier, his father already owned a range of assets in real estate all over Hong Kong. This made sure that he made a fat amount collecting property rent. Moreover, he earned a good deal of money from his shows and concerts. With the rent money and his father's income from show combined, the Lees could easily live a lavish lifestyle. But unfortunately for Bruce, his father was a "miser," in his words. But, in reality, his father was a generous man who frequently helped his family and friends. He many times paid the medical bills of his poor friends—who otherwise could not have afforded to pay them.

He sometimes accompanied his father to his shows. It was during one such show that Bruce befriended Siu Kee Lun, whom he fondly called a unicorn. Siu's father, like Bruce's father, was also an actor in the Chinese opera. There was an age difference of three years between the two boys, but it hardly made any difference for Bruce who never lost any fight against Unicorn. He loved fighting.

His habit of picking up fights with the other children was for obvious reasons, a big nuisance for his father.

Breaking sticks over his body as a punishment made little or no difference to him. But, the practice created a rift between the father and the son.

It was his mother who was his favourite of the two parents. It was she who paid his school fees and dealt with the complaints of his teachers. His teachers often told her that he wasn't a regular at the school. He frequently bunked classes to spend time with his friends in the streets. "Bruce never changed his character" recalls his mother, "he kept repeating the same mistakes time and over." Once she asked her son what he would become later in life? "A movie star," young Bruce replied.

From an early age, he exhibited the traits of benevolence and compassion that he had acquired from his father. Once on a sunny afternoon, his mother noticed that Bruce hurriedly ran out of the house barefoot. When she ran behind him out of the house, she saw him helping a blind man cross the street. It was a proud moment for Grace Lee.

The children in the house called him "little dragon" whereas the elders of the family called him "MoSi Tung," which means "never sits still." The only time when he was not running, jumping, and talking was when he was reading a book. He often used to read late into the night in his bed. According to his mother, this probably was the reason why he became nearsighted. Bruce developed nearsightedness at the age of six and had to wear spectacles.

Young Bruce liked playing pranks on his friends and siblings. It was his habit of playing pranks on others that his friends disliked most about him. He many times crossed the limits. One such incident was when he pushed his sister Phoebe into the swimming pool. She almost escaped from drowning. Once, she held his head underwater until he promised to never pull a prank on her again. Since that day, Bruce never entered a swimming pool again.

At the age of twelve, for his senior secondary schooling, Bruce started attending one of the most famous schools in the neighbourhood, "La Salle." It was a Christian missionary school. Most of the students in the school were Chinese Catholics. Since the first day, he started grabbing the attention of his teachers and classmates for the wrong reasons. All his teachers considered him a "tough pupil." But there was a ray of hope called Brother Henry. He was the only teacher among all who realised a need to channel Bruce's energy into something constructive. He engaged him with cleaning the blackboard, running errands, etc. Bruce did as he asked him to.

Although Bruce was an avid reader at home, he never showed much interest in school. He showed little interest in art and history. And it was biology that he detested the most.

Years of colonial suppression at the hands of British had given rise to malice in the hearts of young, free generation of Hong Kong towards their colonial oppressor. They grew up listening to stories of the atrocities committed by the English on their ancestors. Some anti-Britain groups sprouted all over Hong Kong. Such groups fanned hatred against the British citizens living in Hong Kong. Bruce Lee was the leader of one such gang in his school. To demonstrate their anger and hatred for the British, they would often go and stand outside the King George V School where studied the British children. Bruce and his gang threw abuses, and sometimes even stones at them to instigate them for a fight. If all these measures went in vain, then they would climb the school's fence and mock the children playing in school's playground. Many times, the gang succeeded in commencing a fight, but rarely managed to win them. The pupils of King George V School were way bigger in age and size than Bruce and his gang. Police were often called in to break up the fights. It was his father who had to apologise to the police for his son's juvenile act. Back at home, Bruce had to go through a long session of beating at his hands. Sometimes when he would return home with a black eye, he would talk to no one in his house but run straight to his bed, hoping that his father doesn't find out or that his mother forgets to tell his father, which she sometimes did, intentionally.

More than an angry father, a child fears an absent father. His father was rarely home to express his anger, which had a strong effect on Bruce during his growing up years. To combat the absence of one's father, a child develops either of the two mechanisms. Either it becomes depressed or either it resolves to become more successful than its father. Bruce chose the latter. His father was a successful actor, and martial artist, Bruce in his heart resolved to become a bigger and more successful actor and martial artist than his father. And as the history remembers, he did beat his father in this domain.

❑

The Rise of an Actor

Bruce Lee's romance with the world of cinema began when he was three months old. In a movie called "Golden Gate Girl," he played the role of a baby carried by his father in one of the scenes. He played his first full-fledged role in a movie at the age of six in a movie called "The Birth of Mankind." In the film, he played a kid who fights with another boy of his age, played by his best friend, Unicorn. His first major role came a few months later when starred in one of the top Cantonese TV shows of its time, Chow Sui. He played the role of a wise kid who worked in a factory in Hong Kong. His character was called Lee Siu Lung (The Little Dragon).

In his early roles, he mostly portrayed the role of an orphan or a street urchin. At a later age, he began playing a juvenile derelict or a teenage rebel. Often there were fight scenes in those movies, and he had already developed his style of fighting with some trademark moves such as brushing down the jacket sleeves, slow gaze, wiping the thumb across the nose, and the admonishing finger. He had formal training of "t'ai chi," which is an art of street fighting, from his father. Sometimes, he flawlessly incorporated the moves of 't'ai chi' in his fighting scenes. As a child actor, he appeared in about twenty films. His most appreciated role was in the movie "Orphan" where he played his first and only lead role as a child actor. He matured immensely as an actor through his every role.

Motion pictures were introduced in China in 1896 and the first Chinese movie, "The Battle of Dingjunshan," was released in movie theatres in 1905. In the first few decades, the Chinese film industry was centered in Shanghai. The year 1930 is considered to be the "golden period" of Chinese film industry. A year later, in 1931, after the Japanese invasion of China and the occupation of Shanghai, the film industry in the city was harshly abridged, with filmmakers moving to Hong Kong, Chongqing, and other places. After the shift to Hong Kong, the movies made were centered on the lives in western neighbourhoods of Hong Kong and Shanghai. There were no attempts made to portray the life in the mainland on the silver screen. The martial art movies were rife with the added special effects to enact a scene where the protagonist made about fifty 50 somersaults in the air or made a more than hundred 100 meters jump from one building to another. The film industry lacked innovation and creativity, but this all was about to change with the release of a film made on the life of a martial arts master called Wong Fei-hung, who lived between 1847 and 1924. Wong taught the "Hung Gar" style of "Kung Fu" and was also known to practice herbal medicine. The film was directed by Hu Peng, who insisted on abstaining from using special effects to enact fighting sequences and preferred to show real fighting scenes in the movie. It was the first time that the audience experienced a real fighting scene, with no special effects.

The character of Wong Fei-hung in the movie was played by an actor named Kwan Tak-hing, who was a friend of Bruce's father. Kwan Tak, like Bruce's father, was a well-trained martial artist. And much like the character he portrayed in the movie, he also excelled in Hung Gar style of Kung Fu. Moreover, he had also mastered the Shaolin style of fighting, the one based on the moves of the animals. His movies were based on the philosophy of "Martial Virtue". He and his movies greatly influenced young Bruce. From the year 1950 to 1960, his movies were a huge hit at the box office and had amassed a huge fan following, including Bruce Lee. Bruce could recite every dialogue of his every film made during this period.

❑

The Kung Fu – Game of Fight

Kung Fu means workman, the man who works with art, to exercise one's self-bodily, the art of the exercise of the body applied in the prevention, or the treatment of disease, the singular postures in which certain Taoists hold themselves. The expression "Kung Fu," labour or work, is identical in character and meaning with the word "Congou," referred in the south to a certain kind of tea. In China, it is applied medically to the same subjects as are expressed by the German "Heil Gymnastik," or curative gymnastics, and the French "Kinesiology" or science of movement (An excerpt from "Kung Fu" by John Dudgeon).

In the 1950s, Hong Kong was beset by extreme poverty, crippling economy, overpopulation, and anarchy.

Thousands fled from communist China in search of a safe haven in Hong Kong, which was then under British rule. The state-funded education was limited to a minority, the rest wandered in streets, often in search of jobs, which were sparse to come by. This led to a large number of youth in the streets, who often in search of easy money and cheap adventure, formed gangs among them. Numerous gangs sprouted all over the Hong Kong, which often fought among themselves for the dominance over different areas. Gang wars were a common scene on the streets. Many of them lead to bloody scuffles. Since the members of such gangs didn't have access to weapons, they mainly fought hand-to-hand combat. Bruce, despite getting admission in a private school, was somehow always drawn to the streets. He formed his small gang, naming it "Tigers of Junction Street."

It was at one of his birthday parties that Bruce for the first time met William Chueng. William Chueng was one of the most reputed street fighters of Hong Kong. He was known among the city folks to practice a unique style of Kung Fu, known as Wing Chun. Bruce approached him at the party asking him to teach him the style. William didn't take him seriously and instead advised him to focus on his acting career.

One day, when Bruce was beaten badly in a gang fight, he demanded to be taught a martial art form, so that he could defend himself better in such fights. Although he had formal training in "t'ai chi" from his father, but the slow moves of t'ai chi were of no use to him. He wanted to be taught the swift moves, the ones with intensity and strength. It was after relentless pestering that his mother agreed to give him money for his training.

After getting money from his mother, he hunted down William Chueng and demanded to be trained at the same school as he did. Since he solicited for long, William could not refuse to show him the way to the Restaurant Workers Union Hall, the place where the classes were held. He then introduced him to Yip Man, the master of the school. Influenced by Bruce's celebrity status, Yip Man happily agreed to take him in.

Once the training started, Bruce completely devoted himself to learning Wing Chun. The devotion soon took the form of an obsession. Other pupils at the school nicknamed him "fighting crazy." At the earlier, Bruce learned the art only for street fighting, but as the time progressed, he soon began to focus on the finer nuances and subtleties of "Wing Chun." Bruce's ability to improvise it in real life, seminal in the world of Martial arts, began showing its early signs during his training with Yip Man. The "Wing Chun" style of Kung Fu, which the young Bruce was learning with extreme devotion and sincerity, was about to be introduced to the world by him.

The term Kung Fu is often used as an umbrella term for many Chinese martial arts in general. It isn't only about martial arts history, as it defines any distinct achievement or refined skill that is accomplished after hard work. In that sense, the actual term Kung Fu can be used to define any ability acquired in such a manner, not just those of the martial arts assortment. Still, Kung Fu is extensively used to define a noteworthy share of the Chinese martial arts in the contemporary world. In this sense, the word is typical of highly diverse martial structures that are somewhat challenging to trace. This rather sets the Chinese arts apart from the popularity of martial arts classifications, where an unblemished ancestry is often known.

Martial arts set its foot in China for about for the same reasons as it did in every other society: to help in hunting activities and to defend oneself against the enemies. Apart from this, the signs of martial techniques, including those tied to weaponries and militaries can be traced back to thousands of years in the history of China. The country's Yellow Emperor Huangdi, who ruled in 2698 B.C. commenced solemnising the arts. History says he even invented a form of fighting taught to the army. The fighting involved the use of horned helmets called Horn Butting or Jiao Di. Eventually, it was enhanced upon to embrace joint locks, strikes, and blocks, and it also became a sport during the Qin Dynasty (approximately 221 B.C.).

It is also important to understand that the Chinese martial arts have long held philosophical and spiritual significance within the culture. Apart from this, the martial arts grew along with the ideas of Confucianism and Taoism during the Zhou Dynasty (1045 B.C. - 256 B.C.) and elsewhere, not in seclusion from them. For example, the Taoist idea of Ying-Yang, the universal contraries, found its way to being related in a large way to the hard and soft methods that make up what is Kung Fu. The art also developed along the models of Confucianism, as they were secured to the ideal practices people must practice.

That's why it is very important to talk about Buddhism regarding Kung Fu. Buddhism came to China from India as the relationships between the two countries nurtured during the years 58–76 A.D. In agreement with this, Buddhism grew more and more prevalent in China as the monks travelled to and fro between the countries. An Indian called Bodhi Dharma is chiefly cited in the history books of martial arts. He preached to the monks at the lately moulded Shaolin Temples in China and managed to have altered not only their faculties of thinking by nurturing the ideas such as self-effacement and self-control, but also may have essentially qualified the monks with the martial arts movements.

Though the idea is dubious, what looks clear is that once Bodhi Dharma arrived in China, the monks became famous martial arts experts who toiled tremendously hard at honing their craft. Meanwhile, at the same time, the

Taoist monasteries in the country also sustained different training styles of Kung Fu.

Initially, Kung Fu was only an exclusive art practised by those in power. Thanks to the occupations by the Japanese, and subsequent invasions by the French, and the British, the Chinese started to buoy up the martial arts specialists to open their doors and teach the art form to the native masses to exorcise the foreign invaders. Unluckily, the masses soon realised that the martial arts could not resist the bullets of their enemies.

Years later, Kung Fu found a new adversary in the face of Communism. When Mao Zedong finally took hold of China's power, he tried to abolish almost everything that was customary to build a specific brand of Communism, his brand of Communism. Kung Fu books and Chinese history, including most of the literature on the art at the Shaolin Temple, was put under attack and in many cases wrecked during his rule. Apart from this, many Kung Fu teachers fled the country till the Chinese martial arts, like in earlier times, again became a part of the mainstream Chinese culture once again some years later (in this case, communist nation).

Out of a range of martial styles, Bruce specialised in the Wing Chun. Wing Chun is the name of classification of martial arts established in southern China about 300 years ago. Its inventor, the Buddhist holy sister, Ng Mui, was a teacher of Shaolin Kung Fu and used her expertise to carve a way to take gain of the feebleness intrinsic to the other Shaolin structures. This new system was well guarded and passed on to a small number of students. After some time, this style became famous by the name Wing Chun, named after Ng Mui's first student, a woman named Yim Wing Chun. In 1949, Yip Man, who was considered to be the grandmaster of contemporary Wing Chun, brought the style out of China into Hong Kong and ultimately to the rest of the world.

The main idea of Wing Chun is that the shortest distance between points is measured on a straight line. Unlike t'ai chi, where kicks are made in large circles, in Wing Chun, kicks are made in closer and smaller circle, which makes them quicker in comparison to the kicks in t'ai chi.

The Wing Chun moves take the straightest path possible to the enemy based on the idea that the shortest possible distance between any two points is a straight line. The principal targets lie in the centreline, which is an imaginary perpendicular line intersecting the opponent's vital body parts like—throat, heart, stomach, and groin. A Wing Chun knock is carried centrally from the opponent's chest instead obliquely from the shoulders, as practised in other martial arts forms. This technique helps one learn the centerline concept of Kung Fu. Whereas, in the other martial arts forms, the punch is made obliquely from the shoulder to the centerline. The reason behind the approach is that the distance is shorter when one brings the hand from the shoulder to the center of the chest, and then down the centerline towards the opponent.

One of the most crucial aspects of Wing Chun is the concept of "chi sao," or "sticking hands." It is the term used for the principle and the drills used in the development of instinctive reflexes upon contact and the notion of "sticking" to the enemy. In Wing Chun, it is practised through two specialists maintaining contact with one another's forearms while performing the techniques, thus preparing each other to detect changes in the bodily mechanics, force, thrust, and "touch". This augmented compassion gained from this exercise helps an expert attack and stand an opponent's actions accurately, rapidly, and with the suitable method. Chi jerk or "sticking legs" consist of predefined leg-centered movements, which are executed in a manner akin to Chi Sao.

The Chi Sao training consists of three stages. Each stage requires the practitioner to make progress from the predefined moves to random moves, and at the advanced stage, one has to practice blindfolded. One needs to keep in mind that the moves of Chi Sao rarely apply to real combat situations, but they help develop coordination and awareness, which are the most important aspect of martial arts. It was Chi Sao that gave Bruce Lee his first experience of the interacting forces of Yin-Yang.

The philosophy of Yin and Yang was derived from the age-long reflection of nature, labels the way everything in the universe naturally group themselves in the pairs of contraries—sun and moon, winter and summer, heaven and earth, up and down, night and day, male and female, inside and outside, movement and inactivity.

The following words are drawn from the section "appended remarks" found in the Chinese classic text of I-Ching. "One Yin and one Yang, constitute what is called Tao"; "when Yin and Yang are united in their virtue, the soft and the hard attain their physical shape." Since they were spoken more than two thousand years ago, they became the abstract groundwork for the two great philosophical schools of China, i.e. Taoism and Confucianism. For both these schools, the idea of Yin and Yang, two conflicting yet equally compensating modules establish unity in harmony.

The philosophy of Yin-Yang is used to explaining the mechanism in which nature creates a third force—a force that diffuses through the universe and constitutes a vital force in every living being—also called in ancient Chinese philosophy as "Ch'i." Ch'i is the vital most theory of Chinese philosophy and culture. The philosophy finds its roots in many Chinese traditional religions, but mainly in Taoism and Confucianism. Ch'i literally means "air" or "breath," but as an idea, it refers to the energy flow or life force that is considered to permeate the universe. However, the notion of ch'i has always been debated in the Chinese thinking. Some Chinese philosophers believe that it is a separate force from the physical world, while many think that it comes from the physical matter.

Bruce, after coming home from school, rushed straight to Yip Man's class. On his way to the class, he practised and tried new moves, much to the delight of the passersby. He didn't stop at home either. He continued trying the moves he learnt in the class until he was put to sleep by his mother.

It was one day that his older pupils told Yip Man that Bruce Lee easily defeats them in the fights, and they were pretty angry about it. They thought that he was teaching him something secretively that they did not know about it. Also, they wanted to be taught the same that Bruce was being taught. It was then that Yip Man realised that Bruce Lee was serious about Kung Fu and he had a bright future awaiting him.

❏

Moving to America

Only a year after starting to learn Kung Fu, he developed an interest in dancing. He began learning the cha-cha-cha at a local dance school. He often visited the school with a fellow Wing Chun student named Victor Kan. Bruce started learning dancing mainly to impress his girlfriend called Pearl Cho.

He made his first serious girlfriend in Amy Chan who would later become famous in the Eastern film industry by the name of Pak Yan. The two would often go dancing at the local club. Bruce used to dress-up sharply, in the clothes ironed by himself, for the dates with Amy. She found him funny and kind. But often in the presence of other people, he became too high to handle.

With growing age, Bruce was finding it more and more difficult to control his emotions like anger and frustration. He also had a tough time learning the nuances and subtleties of Chi Sao. It was a troubled period for him. He often got into fights with other gangs. Despite carrying weapons like a blade and a knife, he never used them. Most of his fights involved a broken nose and black eyes with punches and kicks. And moreover, almost all of them involved a visit to the police station for his mother to rescue her son.

In one of the gang fights, he hit his opponent so bad that both William Chueng and his mother had to rush down to the police station to save him. A part of the blame for his handedness of handling the situations goes to hot-headedness, and a part of it goes to his master Yip Man who asked his pupils to try out their moves in the real world. Yip Man also advised calmness and patience to his students, two of the qualities Bruce were never able to acquire. Bruce was not able to take defeats, even if they came once in a while.

One day, Yip Man advised him to stop training for a while and to reflect upon himself. Tired of his aimless wanderings in life, Bruce took his advice and stopped training for some time. He used the spare time to ask himself the important questions like "Why this style?" or

"Why Kung Fu?" After some time, he stopped his pursuit for answers to his questions and returned to doing what he did best, Kung Fu.

Jealous of his rapid success, many of his juniors, when they came to know about his German ancestry, used it as an excuse to boycott him from the school. Banking on Yip Man traditionalist approach, they hoped to expel him from the school, but when this did not work, and Yip Man simply refused to send him out, they protested strongly by refusing to fight and practice along with him. At this point, Bruce got tired of all the hostility that he was facing at the school. Hence he decided to call it a day and to quit training with Yip Man. He then went on to train with a senior student of Yip Man named Wong Sheung Leung and subsequently with William Chueng. Wong Sheung had a small group of students whom he taught. Bruce often falsely told the group that the class was cancelled so that he could get all the time and attention of Wong Sheung by himself.

At the high school, St. Francis Xavier, he was encouraged by one of his teachers, Brother Edward, to participate in the 1958 interschool boxing championship. He happily agreed to participate in the championship and trained hard for the same with William Chueng. He easily sailed through the preliminary rounds, knocking down his opponents in less than three rounds. In the finals, he was facing the three-time champion, Gary Elms, an English boy, from the rival school. Hence, he was carrying an immense burden of expectations of his schoolmates and teachers on his shoulder. In the first few rounds, he suffered some major blows at the hands of his opponents who boxed in the classic style. But, later, he managed to block his other blows using the techniques of Wing Chun and later, applying the same techniques, he knocked out his opponent by the end of third round.

The championships and street fights went hand in hand in his life. The visits to the police station only augmented in numbers. He barely managed to stay afloat at the school and often forced the other students to do his homework. His mother soon started worrying about her son's future. The family then decided to send him away to America. Bruce resisted the idea of immigrating to States, but when his parents insisted, he could not refuse. His mother believed that a prospect of a secure future lay for her son only in the United States.

He told Hawkins Chueng, William Chueng's son about his decision of moving to the United States. He told him that his father didn't like him, and his family didn't respect him, and that he had to earn some respect for himself. He told him that although his family wanted him to become a dentist in the United States, he'd rather make his living by teaching Kung Fu. To this, Hawkins reminded him that he only knew Wing Chun only till until the second form. He lacked what they called in the world of martial arts, the showy moves. His words made sense to Bruce, and he decided to add some "showy moves" to his arsenal before moving to States. He then traced down a man who went by the name of Uncle Siu and taught the northern style of Kung Fu. The two struck a deal. Uncle Siu would teach him two northern style Kung Fu forms, and he would give him dancing lessons. Much to Uncle Siu's dismay, Bruce learned the moves only in three days contrary to his expectation of three weeks. By this time, he could only manage to learn only the basic cha-cha-cha steps.

Bruce remained friends with Unicorn all through his youth. The two worked in movies together during their childhood. Unicorn now was working as an actor in the film industry. The production that had signed him for their next venture had also offered a role to Bruce in the movie. When Bruce discussed the possibility of staying back and working in the film industry with his parents, they showed utmost dissatisfaction. His parents were assured that their son's future laid in the United States. He had to say no to the offer with a heavy heart.

To leave for the United States, he needed to get his clearance from the local police. But Bruce found his and

Hawkins's name in the list of suspected gangsters. He had to get his name cleared from the list to leave the country. He made efforts to get his name cleared but only failed. Days later, it was William Chueng who bribed the police officials to get his son's and Bruce's name cleared from the list so that his son could go to Australia and Bruce to America.

Bruce stayed in the country long enough to become the Crown Colony Cha-Cha-Cha Champion of 1958. Later next year, he said goodbye to his friend Unicorn before leaving for America. His mother slipped about 100 dollars in his hands and his father another fifteen. He then bid adieu to his family members and on April 9, set on a three-week sail through the Pacific to San Francisco, America. Though he had the ticket for the third class, he slept for most of the time in first class as he gave dancing lessons to the first class passengers all through the journey. The only thought that crossed his mind all through the journey was what he was going to do once those 115 dollars ran out?

❏

Finding Ground at Uncle Sam's

Eighteen years later, Bruce returned to the city of his birth—San Francisco. There he put up with his father's friend. Meanwhile, he struggled to find a means of living for himself. He gave dancing lessons at the local dancing club, earning himself small pocket money, enough to get through the week. He also, occasionally, gave impromptu Kung Fu display at the club. There he grabbed many eyeballs, including one of the younger brothers of the owner of the local karate school. But Bruce did not get to spend much time at San Francisco to bask in on his newfound popularity. He soon received a letter from his mother asking him to move to Seattle at one of his father's friend, Chow Ping's house.

During his last days at San Francisco, he was joined by his brother Peter who was on his way to join the University of Wisconsin. Peter sometimes saw his brother kicking, punching, and babbling in his sleep. His inner conflict often took hold of him during his sleep. Soon after Peter moved to the University of Wisconsin, Bruce left for Chow Ping's in Seattle.

Chow Ping, back in Hong Kong, had worked with Bruce's father at the Cantonese Opera Company. Stuck by an illness, he was impelled by the necessity to stay at New York while America joined the Second World War in 1941. It was during his days at the local hospital that he met his future in the face of his nurse, Ruby Chow. The two, after their marriage, moved to Seattle.

Ruby Chow was known by the nickname "Iron Lady" in the neighbourhood. She earned the title after years of struggle against the society and custom to fend for herself and her family a good life, which she liked to live on her terms. She was known for her bold choices in life. She married Chow Ping after divorcing her first husband, which was against the customs of the community. Then she went on to start the first Chinese restaurant outside Seattle's Chinatown, which didn't go well with her community either. But, very soon, her restaurant became a hit in the city's upper circle. She often helped the immigrants from China and Hong Kong with lodging, papers etc. in return for their free labour at her restaurant. Bruce was no different for her than another immigrant. Whereas, he was expecting a guest stay at his uncle, Chow Ping's house.

On being confronted with the reality, he found it hard to grasp it for the first few days. It was for the first time in his life that he found his name on the work schedule. He was given a dingy cell like other workers and was put to work in the restaurant as a waiter. But even there, he managed to find a fair share of fights with the customers and his co-workers. He was not on good terms with Ruby Chow either.

The two frequently confronted each other, accusing one another of charges such as disrespect and exploitation. But neither of the two were ready to give up on each other. It was as if both of them were looking at a reflection of each other in the mirror.

He spent his days studying and working at nights. His mother sent him some money at occasions. Besides, he also worked part-time putting leaflets in the newspapers. After having saved enough, he enrolled himself at the Edison Technical High School. Remember, those were the times when education was mostly state-funded in the United States.

But amidst all the chaos and struggle in life, he did not stop practising Wing Chun. He got himself a Wing Chun wooden dummy shipped from Hong Kong. In 1960, when the Seattle hosted the annual "Asian Culture Day,"

Edison College asked Bruce Lee to put on a Kung Fu demonstration, representing the college. Sitting in the crowd was James DeMile, a former Heavyweight boxing champion for the US Airforce, and a street fighter. Bruce started the demonstration by talking to the crowd about the long kept secret of Chinese culture, which he was going to reveal that day. Then he laid his eyes on DeMille and said, "You look like you can fight. How about coming up here?"

DeMille gave a good look to Bruce as he smiled at his less than 5'7 long and 140 pounds heavy opponent. Bruce then invited him to attack. Intending to land a heavy blow on his jaw, DeMille advanced towards Bruce with a strong punch. Much to his surprise, Bruce easily defended himself from the punch as he blocked it with his wrist. Then DeMille tried several other moves in his book, only to be blocked by Bruce. Then as he stood tired and helpless before him, he swiftly moved his wrist only to stop before DeMile's face. At the end of the fight, as the crowd cheered for Bruce, DeMille asked him to teach some of his moves. Also sitting in the crowd at the time was the African- American Judophile, Jesse Glover. He stood awe inspired by the display and was delighted to know that Bruce studied at the same college as his.

Soon Bruce began teaching Kung Fu in the neighbourhood. Among his students were many judo students, men twice of his age, DeMille, and Jesse Glover.

The classes took place in some backyard or some garage. Later Bruce began taking classes at Ruby Chow's parking lot after finishing his work at the restaurant.

DeMille was friends with Japanese-American named Takayuki Kimura who owned a supermarket in the town. Takayuki moved to America during the time of Second World War. He had previously trained as a Judo master. Thinking that he would be interested knowing about the new Karate Kid in town, DeMille invited him to visit Bruce's classes. Initially not finding the proposal for his use, Kimura restrained himself from visiting, but after being constantly persuaded by DeMille, he decided to pay a visit. On his visit, he found himself mesmerised by Bruce's flair and techniques. And more than the swiftness of his moves, what interested him the most about Bruce was his ability to infuse the Taoist and Confucian philosophy in the middle of the training session. He could not resist the temptation of joining the classes.

In the beginning, Takuki didn't find much common ground with him apart from the classes. But Bruce kept pushing him to spend more time with him after all the two belonged to the same continent. After days of uneasy attempts at starting a conversation, Bruce managed to strike a chord with Takuki, and the two started talking with each other on a daily basis after the classes. The discussions with him proved to be of immense help for Takuki who was facing a midlife crisis. Bruce made him realise his self-worth as a human and as a Japanese immigrant.

Bruce made a girlfriend, in Amy Sanbo—a Japanese immigrant. The two often discussed long hours about life back in their countries, their plans, and their goals in life. While she appreciated his qualities like determinism and dedication to his art, it did not take her long to understand his immatureness about life. She would listen to him at length, bragging about his classes, Kung Fu, and his goals in life. While for her, he was never ears. At times when she accused him of being a show-off, he would often quote from Taoism and Confucianism. She wanted to be a writer, but he found her choice of profession useless and instead advised her to assist him in his pursuit.

Many of his close acquaintances called him an outright chauvinist. At times, he would fail even to demonstrate the slightest evidence of compassion for others. He often argued that if he could find his way out of poverty, why can't others. He carried his uncompassionate behaviour to his classes too. He never demonstrated any of his moves more than twice, and not even bothered to ask his students if they could grasp it or not. As is always the case in every classroom, there was one student who was continuously failing to understand what his master was trying to teach. He was his close friend Takuki Kimura. Despite repeated pleas for a re-demonstration, Bruce never paid any heed to them. After several attempts, an exhausted and disheartened Kimura decided to call it a quit. To his decision, Bruce replied, "you have potential, but you refuse to recognise it." The words infused a new wave of energy in him. He decided to give it another shot. Training even harder than before, it was not very late that he realised that Bruce was teaching him to be his assistant.

After training with his students for some time, to publicise his classes, Bruce began giving demonstrations at the local television channel. During his demonstrations, he planned everything to go perfect, but to his dismay, never did the things go as planned. There was always some or the other goof up by his students, the repercussions of which they faced after the demonstrations.

He often recalled a story of an old lady to his students to boost their morale up. In the story, the house of an old lady catches fire one day. The most valuable thing to her in the house was an old piano. So, she carried the piano first to a safe place once the house was on fire. After the fire was set down, it took about four young healthy men to move that piano back to its place. The story also explained his source of energy too, which was not in his muscles, but somewhere inside his heart. It was his inner strength that made him defeat the tallest and the strongest of the opponents with only a single kick.

Much like his childhood days, Bruce continued to play pranks on his friends in his adult life too. He bought himself different pairs of coloured lenses. He used to put the one with the impression of blood vessels in them. Wearing those lenses, he used to sit down in some restaurant and order in Chinese. Meanwhile one of his friends pretended to interpret him. This trick many times spooked many waiters to death.

He inhibited multiple shades inside him. At one moment he was playing pranks on others, in another, he was lecturing his friends on Taoism and Confucianism. He changed his personalities depending on the situation and person. His ability to switch between different personalities was often considered one of his biggest assets.

Much like the characters, he was going to play in movies later in life; Bruce was known to have a very strong opinion against the harassment of the weaker by the stronger. He always took a stand against such injustices taking place before his eyes. At one such incident, when he and his friends were walking down the road in the Chinatown, they came across a girl who was being harassed by a bunch of guys in a car. Bruce approached them, asking them to stop harassing her. When one of the boys tried to act smart, Bruce landed him a heavy knock on his face.

Little did he realise that his inner strength, which was going to take him to new heights, also had a darker side to it. Little did he ever try to master it, understand it, or even realise it.

❏

The Inner Conflicts

S everal fights marked Bruce's life, but his biggest fights were with himself. Bruce had episodes of sleep talking since an early age. Many nights he spent kicking and talking to himself in his dreams. He carried an immense amount of energy within, which at times was his biggest boon, and at the other times, was his biggest bane in life.

One of the most misunderstood and misrepresented events of his life in the popular culture was when once at Chow's he fought with a force in his dreams for several minutes. Many associated the event with craft, demonic powers, hallucination, etc. But none of the above explanations managed to comprehend the severity of the event in his life fully. Because after this episode, the world came across a completely transformed Bruce Lee. One explanation is that the episode was a confrontation with his dark inner side. What he was trying to fight that day was nothing but himself, his chauvinism, his anger, and his impulsiveness.

Few months after the event, he finished his schooling with grades good enough for him to secure a seat at the Washington University in Seattle. He started attending college in March, 1961. His first choice of subjects at the University were English, gymnastics, and wrestling, all that he enjoyed learning. But later, with an eye on his career, he took up theatre speech and speech improvement classes at the University too. In later years at the University, he also took up courses in social dancing, Chinese philosophy, drawing, composition, Chinese language, general psychology, the psychology of adjustment, personal health, and leadership. He experienced a rush of ambitions accompanied by a rush of energy to accomplish his new goals and ambitions. Running behind his ambitions in the land of dreams, he would often feel homesick, a feeling which motivated him to write about his life in Hong Kong.

As the days passed by, the attendance at his classes experienced a surge. But he had other plans. Instead of teaching, he was more in the learning mode during his classes. He experimented widely and tried new moves on his pupils. Now that he was putting up bigger public demonstrations, he could no longer afford to be beaten by anyone, as it would bring a heavy dent in his reputation. He was about to embark on a journey which was about to take him to places, a journey where he was about to meet fighters much bigger and much stronger than him, it was only his technique that could help him stay at the top. Hence, he had no other choice but to hone his moves.

His fear of a defeat never came to be true, and several factors were at play, which ensured that he remained the best and invincible throughout his life. The first and foremost being his ability to deconstruct the toughest of the moves or the philosophies into simpler and condensed forms. The second was his ability to retain and process a large chunk of information in the shortest time possible. And last but not the least, the third factor was his high level of motivation. It was this motivation that kept alive his desire to know different kinds of styles, in the pursuit of which he travelled through California and Canada, meeting different Kung Fu masters, and learning about their styles. This experience with different styles and masters made him realise the ineffectiveness of the styles that were being taught across the continent. One problem he found recurring with every style was the inability to help them evolve with time. He found that most of them were too slow to be effectively used in real life and hence as he learned more and more about different styles, the lesser and lesser regard he held for those traditional styles and methods of Kung Fu and never did he shy away from exerting his stand at the platforms he got.

He was very vocal about his dislike for the ancient techniques of fighting and his belief that they are ham-fisted for the real-life situations. At one such instance, when he was voicing his dissatisfaction over the ineptness of such techniques during one of his demonstrations, he faced constant heckling from a Japanese black belt Karate student, Uechi. Despite Bruce's confirmation and assurance that his criticism was not meant to be personal and should not be taken as an act of denouncing any one particular style of martial arts, the heckling from Uechi's end did not stop. After some time, Bruce's patience gave away, and he asked the Japanese to have a hand-to-hand combat with him sometime later. The date and venue were fixed. At the handball court of the local YMCA, the two met, accompanied by a small crowd of spectators. As the referee gave the green signal for it to commence, the Japanese firmed his feet on the ground, taking up the classic forward stance of Karate and Bruce aligned himself in the Wing Chun stance. As the spectators remember it, after the first hit that he faced on his stomach, Bruce finished the fight in less than ten seconds, rendering his opponent unable to move at the end of it.

Few of his pupils had the talent and patience required to make his teachings work. Unlike other Kung Fu teachers, he did not offer a crash course in Kung Fu or an easy way to do it. His methods demanded extreme dedication and hard work, a commitment that only few could make.

Allen Joe, a famous martial artist of his times, came to know about this promising upcoming martial artist called Bruce Lee, and he was filled with unbearable curiosity of getting to know him better. Hence, he tracked him down to Ruby Chow's restaurant. That day, he waited patiently, ordering dishes after dishes and enjoying his scotch to meet him. At last, when the two did meet, he showed him some of his moves. To this, Bruce smiled a little and showed him the techniques to block his every move. Impressed by his dexterity, Allen Joe finally asked him to share with him his methods of practising Kung Fu. To this, Bruce showed him the wooden dummy he had imported from Hong Kong, on which he practised his moves, and which he had named after the Buddhist monk Bodhi Dharma.

Not only through his fighting moves, but Bruce exerted his charisma using his words too. On a summer morning, when a twenty-year-old Bruce, arrived as a guest lecturer of Chinese Philosophy at Garfield High School, hand in hand with his then girlfriend Amy Sanbo, he sure turned quite a few heads. One of those heads was that of the seventeen-year-old Linda Emery.

He and Amy had been dating for three years. On several occasions, he proposed marriage, but only to be turned down. In the summer of 1963, he was planning to tell about his relationship with Amy to his family back in Hong Kong. That year, Amy was offered a job in New York and was pondering over the question whether to take it or not. However, Bruce wanted her to turn down the offer and marry him instead. He proposed her for the marriage one last time, offering her his grandmother's ring in the proposal.

Amy turned down his proposal, again.

❑

Vacationing in Hong Kong

In the summer of 1963, a heartbroken Bruce decided to visit his family in Hong Kong, which then consisted of his mother, father, his sister Agnes, brother Robert, a cousin, and an aunt, a servant, and a chicken. His student and his friend Doug Palmer had been taking Mandarin lessons at the University, and hence the thought of refusing the offer of accompanying Bruce to Hong Kong did not cross his mind, not even once.

But little did he understand that it is Cantonese that they spoke in Hong Kong, not Mandarin. As two major dialects spoken in China, the variance between Mandarin and Cantonese is a fascinating topic for a linguist. The official language of China is Mandarin, which is also one of the few official languages at UN also. Though, it is one of the five main languages in central China, which also includes Cantonese. It is often labelled as an offshoot of Mandarin, but the fact that there are blatant variances between Mandarin and Cantonese validates the assertion of Cantonese being a distinct, separate language. One exceptional thing about Mandarin and Cantonese is that they both are the tonal languages and a single term may have several connotations contingent on the context and pronunciation. However, Cantonese is harder in this respect, having 9 tones while Mandarin has 7 tones. Notwithstanding similar typescripts being in used in these languages, the articulation of the words is so disparate that amusingly people describe it as chicken talking to ducks.

Once in Honk Kong, Bruce and Doug never ran out of interesting things to do. The duo tried a long range of activities that summer. They went swimming at the sandy beaches of Hong Kong, movies on the weekends, amusement parks, dined at fancy restaurants, and took a stroll through the lively streets of the city. On quite a few occasions, Bruce played his practical jokes at public places, much to the amusement of the two. They often worked in a team, and their favourite target was the police officers.

When not practising, Bruce liked to dress up in a geeky way, wearing big glasses and loose pants. People on the street often took him for a nerd. His dressing style made him the favourite target of the street goons. Once, when Bruce and Doug were returning from one of the islands in a ferry, two hoodlums started making fun of him. He ignored them for some time, and a few minutes later, knocked one of them down with a punch. The other stood perplexed.

While in Hong Kong, Bruce looked to spend some time with his former trainer Yip Man. He advised Doug to not to reveal before Yip Man that he could do Kung Fu as it could hurt his traditionalist beliefs, which demand him to teach martial arts only to the Chinese. Yip Man and Bruce soon started practising for long hours at the top of his apartments. The two would practice for long hours, starting in the morning and lasting till late in the evening.

After reaching Hong Kong, the first person Bruce searched for was his childhood crush Pak Yan, who now was a star in the Cantonese film industry. The two used to go on frequent dates. During his stay in the country, he helped Pak Yan prepare for several roles in the movies.

Weeks before leaving for Seattle, his father asked him to get himself circumcised. Astonishingly, he agreed to it. He underwent an operation, which that in his words was "extremely painful." For weeks after the operation, he avoided wearing tight pants and only preferred the loose trousers. "Had I known that it would be so painful, I would have never agreed to it." He abstained from practising Kung Fu until the pain vanished.

On their way to Seattle, Bruce and Doug made a stop at Hawaii. At Hawaii, they were asked to give a demonstration at a local school. A big crowd attended the demonstration. A man, standing in a corner and smoking cigarette, was watching the demonstration very keenly. He walked up to Bruce and asked a few questions. Then he asked him to block one of his moves, which Bruce easily blocked. When Bruce left him, he immediately snapped his fist towards Bruce saying, "You left an open space." To this, Bruce, however amused, didn't react. Later, when the same man tried to show Bruce his another move, Bruce, after blocking his move, held him between his fists, making him knock out his cigarette.

On returning to the United States, he realised that the country's government had other plans. He was asked to join the war in Vietnam. He was sent for the physical exam, where, thankfully, he was declared unfit.

That year, Linda Emery graduated from the school, where Bruce once went as a guest lecturer. She started attending the same university as Bruce. Bruce at that time was pursuing his major in philosophy. One afternoon, she accompanied her Chinese friend, Sue Ann Kay, who took Kung Fu classes from Bruce to one of the practice sessions taking place in Seattle's Chinatown. The sessions were being held in a rusty basement.

Soon Bruce's Kung Fu classes were becoming a hot topic among the students at the University. Linda Emery too joined as a student too. His classes were becoming more and more popular as everybody looked forward to them after the day at the university. Bruce then asked the University for the Permission to hold a demonstration at the university's men's gym. The demonstration was an instant hit. The numbers at this classes soared to a new high.

One day after the classes, he asked took Linda out for dinner.

❑

Going to the Chapel

Linda Emery was Bruce Lee's new girlfriend. The fact that Bruce liked to talk, and she was a good listener, made them the perfect match for each other. He was still putting up at Chow's and was looking for a place to move out and start his classes afresh. The inspiration behind his act was Linda. It was her who brought up the idea of Bruce moving out and starting his classes in a rented space.

After going through newspaper advertisements for spaces available on rent, Bruce finalised on the ground floor of an apartment building situated on "4750 University Way." The building was not very far from the University unlike Chow's where students often complained of having to travel a long distance to come for the classes. He fixed the charges for the classes at four dollars/ week. With this, he could support his needs and pay the rent comfortably. On October 1963, Bruce handed over the notice to Chow's and opened his new institute, which he named "Jun Fan Gung Fu Institute."

The new space came preinstalled with showers, but unfortunately not with windows. Bruce and some of his students furnished it with the things he had brought back from his summer trip to Hong Kong. Those things, in a way, gave the place an authentic Chinese touch.

Once the classes commenced at the new place, Bruce and Linda started spending more time with each other. Linda had kept the relationship secret from her parents who were devout Protestants and only wanted their girl to marry in the faith same as theirs; however, she, in her heart, was ready to face the repercussions if they were ever to know about it. During the time they dated in secret, Linda, quite a few times, popped up the question of their future to Bruce. In response to them, he only smiled.

In December 1963, he along with Doug Palmer gave a demonstration at the Garfield High School. This was the same school from where Doug had graduated a year before Linda. During the demonstration, Bruce was about to show the students the move which that was going to become one of his trademarks in the coming years. He had decided to show them "the one- inch punch."

He started the demonstration with the traditional talk about the history of Kung Fu. He then explained to the students, many of whom were learning Karate, the difference between a Kung Fu kick and a Karate kick. All this talking wasn't of much interest to the students who looked bored to death. He then asked one of the students to volunteer for an act. A tall, strong boy raised his hand. The students, most of whom were half-asleep, woke up and seemed to became curious. He then told the students that he was going to punch the guy from a mere distance of "one inch." He then asked Doug to put behind the guy a chair. He leaned back and stretched his hands towards the guy, with his fist tightly closed. He then, in a flash, punched him in the chest, and he went flying backwards, landing on the chair.

Those days, Bruce was in constant touch with a Kung Fu teacher based in Oakland. His name was James Lee. In June, 1964, Bruce and James planned to open the second branch of the famous "Jun Fan Gung Fu Institute" in Oakland. By this time Bruce had completely gone out of touch with his studies and had dropped the plans of completing his doctorate in Philosophy from the University of Washington. He accepted James' proposal and started preparing for making a move to Oakland. He sold his car and got his furniture shipped to Oakland. Before leaving for Oakland, he promised Linda that he would marry her once he has earned enough to support a family.

Oakland is the largest city and the county seat of Alameda County, California, United States. It is the third largest city in the whole San Francisco Bay Area, also the eighth largest city in the state of California, and the 45th biggest in the United States. It is a major West Coast port city and the largest city in the East Bay region of the San Francisco Bay Area. It has a population of 419,267 according to the 2015 figures. It acts as a center for trade in the San Francisco Bay Area; the Port of Oakland is the busiest port in the San Francisco Bay, the entirety of Northern California, and the fifth busiest in the United States. The city is located six miles (9.7 km) east of San Francisco. Oakland was incorporated in the United States in 1852.

The Long Beach Convention and Entertainment Center is a convention center located in Long Beach, California. In July, 1964, it hosted the annual Karate Tournament. With a crowd of thousands cheering for the players, an announcement was made that an Asian guy named Bruce Lee was about to put a short demonstration of a traditional martial art called Kung Fu. Donning a simple, black Kung Fu suit and slippers, Bruce entered the arena. He started the demonstration with the one finger push up and ended it with a "one-inch punch" on one of the contestants who flew back and gasped for breath. His purpose of showing the one-inch punch was to demonstrate to the public the more effective and the less energy requiring punching techniques that Kung Fu offered.

Standing on the other end of the punch was the Filipino martial artist, Dan Inosanto. The incident, in his own words, left him flabbergasted. He then made up his mind to train with Bruce and tracked him down to his hotel room.

Dan and Bruce soon became friends and started spending time together at training and bookshops. Dan arranged for Bruce to give demonstrations in the city of San Francisco. As in his other demonstrations, the ones at San Francisco had the similar lighting fast kicks, punches, blocks, etc. Spending time with him, Don Dan learned quite a few of his acts too.

All this while, Bruce and Linda were in constant touch with each other through letters. Very soon, Bruce proposed for marriage, and this time his proposal was accepted. The two decided to get married in secret, move to Oakland, and then inform their parents. On August 12, 1964, Bruce returned to Seattle with a wedding ring in his pocket. Despite their every attempt to keep the marriage a secret from Linda's parents, her aunt came across its details mentioned in the local newspaper, as necessitated by the law. Like any other aunt, she called up Linda's mother, complaining about not receiving the invitation to the marriage. The call left Linda's mother in a state of shock and bewilderment.

The Emerys tried every possible weapon in their arsenal to persuade the couple to call off the marriage. But the revelation that Linda was pregnant with his child had the family making arrangements for the marriage. The venue was decided to be Seattle Congregational Church. Bruce wore a wedding suit rented from a local store and Linda didn't even have a wedding dress to wear. Taky Kimura was the best man at the wedding and also the only person to have been invited from outside the family.

❏

The Winning Fights

Bruce had started the second branch of his Kung Fu school in Oakland in partnership with James Lee. At the time Linda and Bruce tied the knot, Bruce didn't own a house in Oakland, and James Lee and his wife were more than happy to have him and Linda as their guests until Bruce found an accommodation. But within months of them moving in, James Lee's wife died of cancer. She left behind a young son and daughter. Linda started taking care of the children, and James Lee asked Bruce to consider living with them instead of finding another accommodation for him and Linda.

James Lee was twenty years older than Bruce. In the past, he had been a state weightlifting champion, an amateur boxer, and a brown belt in Judo. But as his life turned out, he had to work as a welder to earn a living. James had also trained in traditional Kung Fu, but due to his dislike for the mechanical moves and training approach, he later went on to develop his informal style, incorporating moves of Kung Fu and other martial arts. Bruce and James shared a common view of making Kung Fu less mechanical and more suitable to the needs of a real combat situation.

The two, with this vision, opened the second branch of Jun Fan Gung Fu Institute at the Broadway street in Oakland. The initiative was initially a flop with less footfall, but thankfully, it was funded by the profit earned from the branch in Seattle, which helped it in staying afloat. Bruce never made tall claims in the advertisements he put up for his Kung Fu classes. Unlike other Kung Fu schools in the neighbourhood, he never claimed to teach the art in six months or one year. He didn't want restless students who were in a hurry of learning the art in the least possible time; rather he wanted serious pupils who would be devoted to the cause of learning it with patience. He wanted students who were ready to enter into the spirit of this art form. Hence he refused to teach readymade moves and instead encouraged his students to evolve and create. Just as his classes were beginning to show better attendance, he was challenged for a fight by a new Kung Fu instructor in town who went by the name of Wong Jak Man.

Before Bruce coming to this country, much of the Kung Fu was alive, but most of it was taught to the Chinese community. There was nothing taught to the outsiders. Bruce came along and on the basis of trying to create equality amongst all people regardless of race. He chose to, you know, to let anybody into his school regardless of what colour or race they were from as long as he knew what was in their heart was good and positive. "He took them in and then when he was done in San Francisco, where the Chinese community with much more like being in China they took an exception to it, and he had to fight his way out of it," recalled Taky Kimura in an interview.

Jak Man had recently arrived from Hong Kong with the aim of teaching Kung Fu to the Americans. He was 5' 10" tall and weighed 135 pounds. An expert in Shaolin styles, he also had training in internal Kung Fu styles. To make a name for himself in the Kung Fu scene of the city, he decided to challenge the best Kung Fu teacher in the town, Bruce Lee. He challenged him to a match, and the winner would get to run the school and while the loser will have to stop teaching the martial art.

The date and venue were decided for the fight. Some ground rules, such as no eye jabs, no groin kicks, etc. were set before the fight. As the two men looked at each other, Bruce Lee made a curious remark regarding a friend of

Wong Jack Man's who had helped to set up the fight. He said, "Your friend has killed you."

The floor was cleared, the fighters bowed, and Wong Jack Man moved forward and stretched his hand for the pre-fight handshake. Bruce jumped forward with a quick lance hand to the eyes. Wong was astonished but rapidly developed into his traditional Kung Fu mode of fighting. Bruce, for his part, took a Wing Chun posture. However, when the men were in postures, Bruce was the more aggressive one. For long minutes the fight continued, Bruce unable to finish it, and Wong unable to move off the defensive. Linda Lee claims that Wong was running from one end to other for cover and safety, but Wong's supporters beg to differ. They tried to deter away Bruce, but Jim Lee intervened. The fight was later called off.

"In Oakland, he received a challenge from the San Francisco Chinese martial arts community, and the challenge read that Bruce, if he were to be defeated in this challenge would have to cease teaching Caucasian or non-Chinese students. And the Chinese martial artist came over from San Francisco to Bruce's studio in Oakland, and a very formal challenge took place. I was present there, in fact, I was eight months pregnant with Brandon, and James Lee was there, and this fight with this Chinese martial artist lasted about three minutes. It consisted of a lot of running. The Chinese martial artist took off and started running around the room, and Bruce was pursuing him before Bruce finally got hold of him and took him down to the floor and made him give up. The challenge ended with the Chinese martial artist being soundly defeated and they all went away. Bruce won the right to teach anyone he wanted to," said Linda Lee in an interview.

A highly self-critical man, Bruce was left deeply annoyed and dissatisfied with his performance in the fight. The very fact that it took him more than three minutes to finish the fight left him deeply hurt inside and began thinking ways of improving his punches and kicks. One thing that struck him most was the power lacking in his punches and kicks. He had the technique right, but his ch'i wasn't working up to the mark.

With help from James Lee, he began an intensive physical training course. He began his day meditating for hours. Then he would go on a long run of several miles. His dogs accompanied him during the run. Then after finishing his lunch, he spent hours on the training bike. The evenings culminated with long sessions of sit-ups. Sometimes he also lifted weight to develop his forearms. In no time he had gained more muscles than ever before. To fulfil the need for protein, he included protein shakes and weight gain drinks in his diet. He supplemented his diet with a high dose of vitamins.

"He trained insane," recalls his friend and trainer James Lee. At times, he would not stop until he was out of breath, and once he regained it, he would start again. He never stopped training.

Even when out, he never missed out on any opportunity to practice his moves. He would practice kicks on trees; to master the accuracy of his kicks, he kicked the litter blown by garbage. Those were the times when martial arts wasn't practised by any machine, but Bruce felt an immediate need of it; hence, he and James Lee went on to design and constructed many machines for a martial arts training.

Soon James Lee's garage was filled with all kinds of machines such as a heavy bag for punching; air filled kicking shields, loop and pulley device to stretch legs, etc. Even the old Wing Chun wooden doll that Bruce had imported from Hong Kong was modified as per the needs of his training.

During his training sessions at his institute, he tried every trick to stir up the real emotions of anger and fear among his students to make them fight ready. After months of such intense training and dedication, his punches and kicks reached their optimum level and became deadly enough to send an ordinary person flying in the air. He then resorted to trying his moves only on the wooden dummy as they had become too deadly to be tried by a person. Many holding the kicking bag for him ended up dislocating their shoulder blades.

❑

Before the Big Break

66 **W**ater is the softest substance in the world, and yet it can penetrate the hardest rock or anything. You name it. It is insubstantial. By that I mean, you cannot grasp it or punch it and hurt it. So every Kung Fu man is trying to do that: To be soft like water and flexible and adapt itself to the opponent."

Above is an excerpt from Bruce Lee's first screen test for a part in a TV series about a Chinese detective. How did he land up a screen test? It was out of sheer chance. On August 2, 1964, at Long Beach, California, where Bruce gave a Kung Fu demonstration, he showed the "one-inch punch," and his two-finger push-ups, which that left the crowd awe-inspired. In the crowd was Jay Sebring, the hair stylist for the Batman TV series. He recalled Bruce's genius before William Dozier, a T.V. producer, who was looking to cast a part in a TV series about a Chinese detective. Sebring then showed a film of Bruce's demonstration at Long Beach. An impressed Dozier later asked Bruce to fly down to Los Angeles for a screen test.

On February 1, 1965, in Los Angeles, California, where the 24-year-old Bruce Lee is in the midst of his first audition for a TV series that will never be made. But nineteen months later, this audition was about to lead him to his first break on T.V. as Kato from The Green Hornet.

"And you went to college in the United States?"

"Yes," Bruce replied.

"And what you've done."

"Em, Philosophy."

Wearing a black suit, a white shirt, and a small tie with a knot, Bruce initially exhibited some signs of nervousness. But he was only going to pick up his form. As the questions moved into his domain of expertise, he grew more and more confident with every passing question.

"And you worked in motion pictures in Hong Kong?" asked the interviewer.

"Yes, since I was six years old."

"Now you told me earlier today that karate and jujitsu are not the most powerful and the best forms of oriental fighting. What is the most powerful and the best form?"

"Well it's bad to say the best, but I think Kung Fu is pretty good," Bruce answered.

"Well, you tell us a little bit about Kung Fu."

"It originated in China and is the ancestor of Karate and Jujitsu. It's more of a complete system, and it's more fluid. By that I mean it's more flowing; there is continuity of movement instead of one movement, two movements, and then stop."

"What's the difference between a Kung Fu punch and a karate punch?"

"Well the karate punch is like being hit by an iron bar—WHACK!" He paused for a moment, then smiled and continued, "A Kung Fu punch is like being hit by an iron chain with an iron ball attached to the end of it—WHANG!—and it hurts inside."

America's only experience of the martial arts until 1965 was by far of Judo and Jujitsu, which seeped into the country through Japanese arts that were taught to the soldiers during the Korean War. Bruce considered himself as an ambassador for the Chinese martial art.

In spite of his expertise in Kung Fu, his study of philosophy caused him to question why most martial artists, Chinese and otherwise, looked more apprehensive with preserving tradition then than with looking more deeply into the matter or to pierce through to the eventual truth of martial art. He established his method of Kung Fu, which he described as non-classical and which took as its core the principles of economy of motion, simplicity, and directness.

"For instance, you will read it in a magazine and everything that when somebody grabs you, you will first do this and then this and then and then and then and then thousands of steps before you do a single thing." Bruce continued, "of course this kind of magazine would teach you to be feared by your enemies and admired by your friends and etcetera. But Kung Fu, always involves a very fast motion. It's not the idea to do so many steps, and then you let go. This is what we mean by simplicity. Same thing, in striking, and in everything. It has to be based on a very minimum motion so that everything would be directly the expression of one motion and he is going to do it gracefully not yelling and jumping all over."

Impressed by his belief in Kung Fu, the interviewer then asked him to show some of its moves.

"Show us some moves," asked the interviewer.

"Well it is hard to show it alone, but I will try to do my best," Bruce replied.

Then a volunteer walks in and stands before him to aide Bruce in demonstrating his moves.

"I will go ahead although all accidents do happen," said Bruce before showing his moves.

"There are various kinds of strikes; it depends on what weapon you'll be using," he said while taking a Kung Fu stance.

"To the eyes, you would use fingers," he continued. He asked the volunteer not to worry as he assured him that he'd be unhurt.

"Straight at the face from the waist, and everything on," he enunciated while directing his fist towards the face of the volunteer.

"Let's move another way around. This way, so you're doing it more in the camera," interrupted the interviewer.

"Then there is pen arm strike, using the waist again into the back fist," Bruce continued. "You know that Kung Fu is very sneaky. The Chinese, they always hit low from thigh to the groin."

All his moves were hypnotic for the audience present in the room. And despite the fact that Bruce carried out them at a lesser speed than his normal, many a times they went unseen.

❏

The Jeet Kune Do

By February 1967, Bruce had three Kung Fu schools operating in America. The schools were located in Seattle, Oakland, and Los Angeles. At his schools, he taught his elucidation of the martial art based on his investigations into the decisive truth of this unarmed combat. Nevertheless, by now, the young Bruce was publicly critical of the traditions and limitations he had experienced as an inherent in the martial arts. The form in which they were taught in schools around the world; he found that they lacked a solid grounding in reality and consisted only of rehearsed self-defence routines, most of which were employed in a predictable pattern. From his experience, he understood that the real combat is spontaneous not rehearsed, unlike the way they were taught. He realised that they were made up of irregular and broken rhythms that a martial artist cannot anticipate, but only respond to. In fact, even the karate tournaments of his times were non-contact affairs, mostly decided not on knockouts but on an amassing of points given for blows that never touched the opponent. A team of judges judged the victory. The judgment was made by assuming which combatant would probably have hurt the other combatant the most if in case the contact been were allowed. Bruce found such styles of no use. Such pseudo fighting, which he called organised despair and dry land swimming. His criticism of the art form can be traced to his background in Hong Kong where he often used to be involved in not so codified karate tournaments but in no-rules street fights and challenge matches. These fights and matches were fought on the rooftops in Hong Kong.

As mentioned in earlier chapters, he had also fought frequently against opponents who had been armed with knives, chains, and other lethal weapons. In such encounters, referees and judges were seldom required. Instead of participating in such traditional karate tournaments, he preferred devoting himself to developing a more scientific style to weapon-less fight. His research led him to the science of Newtonian physics and the methods and doctrines of European fencing and western boxing, which were proficiency driven, unlike the Chinese martial arts, which were more traditional in their approach. This research helped him understand that the only litmus test of a combative technique's worth is whether or not it can be landed effectively on an opponent? Everything that was patterned, he discarded it from his style and retained only those techniques that he has was determined to use in a real self-defence situation. He was probably the first martial artist in the world who asked his students to wear boxing gloves, headgear, and body protectors and take it all out. This practice laid for the modern Mix Martial Arts style of fighting. Nothing was planned out. No punches were pulled, and only full-contact reality-based martial art was the order of the day at his classes. In 1967, he introduced the notion of a full contact scuffling at the International Karate Tournament in long beach, California. Defensive moves were not stressed upon in his new reality-based method, or it would have allowed the enemy in the fight to set the tone and tempo of the combat. He in his new style instead focused on attack or more specifically on intercepting the opponent's attack with an attack of one's own. By the mid-summer of 1967, he had decided that the essential characteristic of his new style of martial art would be the principle of intervention. Since a character signifying a fist usually signifies the Cantonese term for defenceless combat, he decided to name his new approach—Jeet Kune Do.

In his book, 'Tao of Jeet Kune Do', Bruce says, "For security, the unlimited living is turned into something dead, a chosen pattern that limits. To understand Jeet Kune Do, one needs to throw away all the ideals, patterns, styles; in fact, he should throw away the concept of what is or what isn't ideal in Jeet Kune Do. Can you look at a situation without naming it? Naming it, making it a word causes fear."

Jeet Kune Do or JKD is the only non-classical Kung Fu system in existence today. Jeet Kune Do takes shape from Bruce Lee's idea to take the best of Wing Chun Kung Fu, American Boxing, French Fencing, and Grappling to bring them together as the ultimate combat art, from the ultimate combat artist. The style was still developing when Bruce Lee died. It is also different from other traditional martial arts because Bruce used his individual experiences and understanding to develop what many now call to be the most popular method of self-defence. Jeet Kune Do also, many times, referred as Mixed Martial Arts.

Bruce believed that an effective self-defence method needs to be simple. His research about different fighting forms indicated him that most martial arts had a lot of reactions to deal with a single form of attack. Also, he established that some martial arts had more than twenty ways of dealing with a specific type of punch, which was often puzzling during a real fight. He then started to work on developing a style with one simple and direct solution. This is the reason behind his liking for the idea of a concurrent block and hit since it simplified countering an attack. He first learned about this idea in the traditional style of Wing Chun and then went on to integrate it with the idea of "stop-hitting," a counter-offensive technique found in the world of Western fencing. It required the practitioner to lead with his/her principal hand. While standing in an attacking position with his strong hand and leg forward, Bruce realised that he could do "Western fencing without the sword," hence he applied the concept of stop hitting into the system of empty-hand. Bruce considered that the best way to stop an opponent's attack is to intercept it with a stop-hit by his strong hand or leg. Thus, in 1967, he named his martial art, Jeet Kune Do—the way of the intercepting the fist.

❏

The Green Hornet

A week after his first screen test for a role in a Chinese detective TV series, the news of his fathers' death broke him down. He had to fly to Hong Kong immediately while Linda stayed back. On arriving at the mortuary where his father was buried, his legs ceased to move. He had to put every effort into his body to be able to walk up to his father's coffin. The traditions demanded repentance from the son who fails to be present by his father's side during his death. One can assume that perhaps his deep sobbing might have satisfied the demands of the tradition.

Two weeks later, Bruce returned to Oakland. A day after his arrival in Oakland, he received a telephone from William Dozier informing him that the series he auditioned for has been shelved, but owing to his excellent audition, he has been selected for another role in a series called Green Hornet.

In May 1965, Bruce and Linda, with their newborn baby, boarded the flight for Hong Kong. He had to settle some real estate disputes over his father's property in Hong Kong. The trip to the country proved more difficult for Linda than she had imagined it to be. At first, the humidity was a nuisance for the child and ultimately for Linda. Sometimes the child cried for hours, giving many sleepless nights to her mother. To add to her woes was the language barrier between her and her in-laws. And on the top of it was the extremely different food preferences. In short, she wasn't prepared for the culture shock she witnessed while in Hong Kong.

During their stay, Bruce was in constant touch with the producers of Green Hornet back in the States. He made regular calls inquiring when was the shooting going to begin. He had even planned to visit Yip Man while he was in Hong Kong. He had a favour to ask for.

He wanted to film Yip Man performing Kung Fu stunts so that he could show it to his students back in America. But like any other conservative Guru of his kind, Yip Man refused to be filmed. Disappointed, he returned home with the feeling of self-reproach over asking him for the favour in the first place. Four months later, he returned to Seattle to live with Linda's family for some time. All this while, he was sitting on his haunches, waiting for the call from the producers. Meanwhile, he waited for the call; he devoted his time to reading the philosophies of several new-world and old-world sages and spiritual gurus of the Oriental world. Of all the philosophers he read, he was influenced most by Buddha, Lao Tzu, and Krishnamurti. Those long sessions of reading took a toll on his back, and he began suffering from backache.

One day, his wait culminated. He received a call from William Dozier informing him that shooting was about to start in three months' time. In March, 1966, he with Linda moved into a small apartment in Los Angeles. He was about to be paid $400 for each episode of Green Hornet.

Green Hornet started as a radio program in the late 1930's and continued through the early 1950's. It is a fictional character, an incognito crime-fighter, created by George W. Trendle and Fran Striker, with input from radio director James Jewell. It started its run on WXYZ in Detroit, the Mutual Network, and NBC Blue in 1936. The duo—George W. Trendle and Fran Striker, had also worked in the past on the radio series named Lone Ranger. The radio series of Green Hornet was dubbed by Al Hodge, Donovan Faust, Robert Hall, and Jack McCarthy in the order. The theme song was "Flight of the Bumblebee," with different noises added in the background.

Green Hornet, with his partner Kato, used martial arts as well different weapons like gas guns to fight crime in the city. They ride around the city in their car, which they call "the Black Beauty." In the earlier radio productions, the character of Kato was described as a Japanese martial artist, but later, after the attack on Pearl Harbour, it was changed to a Filipino. On the radio, Kato was initially played by Raymond Hayashi, then Roland Parker, and in the later years by Mickey Tolan and Paul Carnegie. In the 1966 television series, he was portrayed by Bruce Lee.

Bruce's portrayal of Kato made the series popular in both the United States and Hong Kong, where it was known by the name of "the Kato show." This portrayal of Kato made Kung Fu popular in the mainstream pop culture in the west. Van Williams played the leading role of Green Hornet in the series. The series was discontinued after one season, which had twenty-six episodes in it. Although based on the radio show of the 1930s, of the same name, this televised series was different in many respects. For example, Bruce's character of Kato in the television series used green sleeve darts as an alternated attack for situations in which hand-to-hand combat was either dreadful or too risky. One of the most popular episodes of the series was the one where Kato and Robin were seen fighting each other. The result was a tie. The series has inspired many comic book and movies adaptations over the years and made the character of Green Hornet a part of the mainstream comic world.

For Bruce, Green Hornet was more than his first break on the television screen. It gave him the opportunity to show his talent to the world. For the first time in his life, he was able to show what he had been practising almost his entire life before such a large audience. The series made Kung Fu and Bruce Lee the household names in Hong Kong and America. And little did anyone know that in the coming years, the two words were going to become synonymous with each other, breaking barriers and reaching new heights in the company of each other.

❑

The Tryst with Hollywood-I

In February, 1967, Bruce went on to open his third Kung Fu training school at 628 College Street in the Chinatown district of Los Angeles. It was only a few blocks away from the famous Dodger Stadium. He liked having absolute privacy in his schools. Hence, he painted the windows black and located it in a remote corner where it did not attract any attention. He now taught more than 50 students under one roof, and the number was only increasing day by day. It was getting tougher for him to teach all the students together. He needed help. Hence, he appointed Dan Inosanto as his assistant. He then limited the membership to the school only to the previously trained martial artists who exhibited talent.

Bruce showed different sides of his personality during the training. At times he could be relaxed and calm, and at other, tensed and strict. He changed his mood as the situation demanded. At one point, when the interactions between him and the students became too informal and undisciplined for him, it prompted him to take the required measures. He asked his students to stop referring him by his name and instead show some respect and call him "Sifu," the Chinese word for master.

Unlike his days with Yip Man, when he tested his patience and dedication for months, he found such an exercise both futile and unnecessary. He found it distant from reality. He constantly sought detachment from traditional teaching styles of Kung Fu, the one under which he was trained.

He used to put a great emphasis on personal fitness and designed a fitness program, according to the needs of every student, for his every pupil. Meanwhile, during his training and teaching, his biggest hurdle was his short temperedness. He very often used to get in fights with his students, almost always hurting them badly. His friend and assistant Dan Inosanto recall, "If Bruce had one drawback, I think it was the temper he had."

But it did not take him long to cool his temper. It used to go away as soon as it came. Displaying the other side of his character, he was quite compassionate at times too. He once bought Dan an expensive set of weights, which he had set his eyes on for quite a time but was unable to buy.

The past repeated itself. Like in Oakland, here in Los Angeles, Bruce was again challenged by two local martial artists for a fight. Learning from his experience with such confrontations, he this time didn't succumb to the temptation of beating the shit out of those two martial artists but smartly turned them down.

To supplement his income, he started giving private tuitions at 50$ per hour. Now he was giving private tuitions to some big names in Hollywood. His list of students included stars like Steve McQueen and James Coburn. Many big names of the Karate world trained too under Bruce Lee's mentorship.

Bruce's tryst with Karate has a long history. Karate was made popular in the United States by the serviceman posted in Japan and Korea during the Second World War and Korean War, respectively. In the 1960s, it was taken to the masses by Ed Parker, the man who organised The Long Beach Tournament, where Bruce gave a spell-bounding demonstration of Kung Fu. But things in the Karate world were changing rapidly. The biggest name in American Karate community, Chuck Norris, had succeeded in mixing Japanese and Korean arts, incorporating the Japanese kicking and Korean punching styles in his style. It only meant that Bruce needed to evolve too, rapidly.

Bruce, when he was not training, was a voracious reader. He had a large collection of books in his library. Most of the books were about some of the other forms of fighting. From boxing manuals to Karate magazines, his collection had it all. As long as the book had anything to do with the fighting, it ended up in his library. He had great respect for those books and considered them as the treasuries of knowledge. Besides the book on fighting, he also had books on archery, ballet, and dancing. He had a vivid taste in philosophy, which reflected well in his library collection. He read philosophies of Chinese philosophers like Confucius and Lao Tzu. There were also the books of Krishnamurti and Khalil Gibran in his library. He even had a collection of videos of some of the biggest fights in the past. His favourite was the boxing match of September 26, 1951, between Willie Pep and Sandy Saddler. He was a big fan of Muhammad Ali and many times used to practice his punches while looking in the mirror.

It was one thing to know him as a teacher, and it was another to know him as a friend. However, in both the roles, he had a charm attached to him, a kind that many referred as magic. His Karate students were some of the biggest names of the American Karate fraternity. They all were already great fighters before they started to train under him. Despite commanding great respect among his Karate students, he only commanded despise and ignorance in the Kung Fu community. The traditional martial arts community in the country only saw him as nobody whose means were little more than excited street fighting. But little did their views effect on him. He continued to defy the traditional norms and rules of Kung Fu during his training.

He stressed on making his training sessions as much like the scenario of actual combat as possible. He taught what was necessary to win the fight. He only used the punches and kicks which that he deemed effective enough for a real fight. His techniques were dismissed as a juvenile by many Kung Fu masters. His principles of "adapt and improvise" found less of acceptance in the Kung Fu world.

The first time he put on boxing gloves, he won himself the interschool championship. Later in life, he fenced with his brother, who was a Commonwealth Games Champion. As we know through earlier chapters, he had also practised the art of t'ai chi with his father when he was young. His expertise lied in Wing Chun, which he practised all his life. Before arriving in America, he added to his arsenal the know-how of other martial arts such as "praying mantis," "eagle claw," and "hung gar." In the States, it was Taky Kimura who introduced him to Judo. He then went on to hone his Judo skills with other Judo artists such as Sato and Jesse Glover. He also tried his hands at Filipino martial arts while practising with Dan Inosanto. He befriended the star wrestler Gene La Belle on the sets of Green Hornet. The two shared the moves of each other's styles. He also had many fruitful encounters and training sessions with the famous Jujitsu artist Wally Jay. Thai boxing, Western boxing, French foot fighting, he had trained in all. Such exposure to almost all major forms of fighting helped him cherry pick the best and most effective moves while he was developing his style.

Although he was training hard, meditation never missed his daily schedule. He meditated daily as he looked for ways to develop his ch'i.

Unlike other Kung Fu masters around him who took a class of hundreds of students in one time, Bruce's professionalism and unconventional teaching methods never allowed him to teach more than a handful of students at one time. Hence, he could not open any more schools. This only meant him having to give more private lessons to keep himself afloat.

Meanwhile teaching in Hollywood, the idea of acting in Kung Fu movie crossed his mind several times. In fact, it was always was at the back of his mind. He even had drawn plans in his minds for a movie about a Shaolin, warrior priest. This priest used his Kung Fu skills to fight crime in the city. He went with his idea to a TV producer named Tom Kuhn who suggested the name "Warrior" for the movie.

Among his celebrity pupils were movie stars like James Coburn and Steve McQueen and the famous screenwriter Stirling Silliphant. Silliphant had heard about his fight with the famous singer Vic Damone's bodyguards, a story that was doing rounds in the social circles of Hollywood.

Vic Damone, a famous singer in the 1950s and 1960s, witnessed his strength—and strategic genius—personally in 1968. Damone, at the top of his fame in the late 1960s, presumed he'd employed the best two-man security workforce that money could buy, and he dared Bruce, to try to get past them. The impression, in agreement with Damone's orders, was to put Bruce "on his ass and teach him a lesson." Bruce, though, proposed to offer a lesson of his own, telling Damone he wished to sidestep his first bodyguard easily, and then buzz a cigarette out of the mouth of the second.

The cigarette, Bruce said, will signify a gun, and the bodyguard had to take it out of his mouth before Bruce's kick could get to it. And all of the moves, from the entry to the kicking of the cigarette kick and reaching to Damone by getting past his bodyguards, was about to happen, according to Bruce, in less than five seconds. The bodyguards, for obvious reasons, didn't believe any of this was possible, and neither did Damone. Bruce had even taken out the advantage of surprise from his act. The bodyguards knew he was coming, and they were ready for him. They mounted by the door, ready to beat him as soon as it opened. The door, nevertheless, didn't open the way they thought it would. In fact, it didn't open at all. It instead blasted off its joints and banged into the first bodyguard with so much of energy that it slumped him out across the floor. Bruce had appropriately anticipated that at least one of the bodyguards would make the error of putting himself too close, so he jerked it open. One down. Then, before the second bodyguard could respond, he foot snapped up to his mouth and thrust his cigarette out of his mouth. It flew past the nose of a surprised Damone. Damone turned back to Bruce, who was now standing an inch away, checking his watch. Four seconds had gone by.

Damone's reaction was about to find reverberation in Hollywood's social circles: "Holy shit."

His popularity and his fees were directly proportional. He first hiked his fees to $100 per hour and then again hiked it to $250 for an hour. The stories of his fights and his expertise reached the ears of one the biggest directors in Hollywood, Roman Polanski. He had him fly to Switzerland for a private lesson.

Back in Hollywood, his celebrity students like Coburn and Silliphant were showing tremendous growth and commitment. Both had made good progress in it and had developed personal bonds with Bruce too.

During the years 1968 and 1969, some of Bruce's students from Hollywood got him small side roles in different movies. He made an appearance in the TV series called Ironsides and Blondie. In the TV series "In Here Come the Brides,"; he played a Chinese monk on screen. He was also hired by different production houses to be the technical advisor and sometimes stunts director. But none of these roles brought him the fame as Green Hornet did. After Green Hornet, Bruce found it almost impossible to be cast in the lead role of any other TV series or movie. In those days, there were not enough roles being written in Hollywood for a Chinese Kung Fu master, except for a few stereotypes. His friend, Stirling Silliphant, who was one of the biggest screenwriters of his time, understood that it required a special script, written with Bruce in mind, to land him the break that he was looking for.

Meanwhile, Silliphant managed to get him involved in the movie 'A Walk in the Spring Rain' as the stunt choreographer. In the movie Marlowe, Silliphant managed to write a role for Bruce, which allowed him to show his athleticism and strength as a martial arts fighter. However, Bruce spent time on screen for only a couple of minutes, but this marked his first appearance in a full-length Hollywood movie.

Meanwhile, Bruce was struggling to find a foot in Hollywood, relying on the income earned from his private tuitions, he found Linda pregnant for the second time. With a growing family, he felt the need to move to a bigger house. He went on to look for a bungalow in the uptown Bel Air locality of Hollywood. After finding it out of his budget, he had to settle for a bungalow at Roscomare Road in downtown. He bought it for about $50,000. It was not very late that he began struggling to pay the instalments of the loan he took to buy the bungalow. He found some relief in the form of money that he received after he sold a piece of his father's property in Hong Kong. But instead of using the money to buy furniture for his new house, he bought himself a new red Porsche and went racing along the Mullhond Drive with Steve McQueen.

Although he took great pride in the fact that all three of the US karate freestyle champions and a bunch of celebrities were training under him, he felt inside him a need to make the shift to movies. The only problem was that the others didn't feel quite the same way. Moreover, no producer was willing to risk his money on an unknown Chinese Kung Fu master.

Bruce realised his limitations very soon. He stopped aiming for the lead roles but now instead aimed for a strong supporting role in a big feature film. He felt that a strong supporting role along with a big star will give him the recognition that he was looking for and ultimately open new doors for him.

He even had an idea for a movie in which he saw himself playing the support to the lead. The movie went by the name of "The Silent Flute." In the movie, the protagonist was to go on a journey where he would face obstacles in the way. His way out lied in the voice of his soul, which was to be played by Bruce himself.

He wanted Steve McQueen to play the lead. He asked Silliphant to work on the script of the movie. One day, Bruce and Silliphant went to Steve McQueen's house to convince him to play the lead. Steve refused with a straight face to play the lead of the movie. Bruce did not utter a word until he moved out. Standing out of Steve

McQueen's house, he vowed to become a bigger star than him.

After being refused by Steve, the two then went to James Coburn who happily agreed to play the lead. After days of inactivity on Silliphant's part which was responsible for developing the script, Bruce became more and more restless. His restlessness reached a new height after the birth of his daughter Shannon on April 19, 1969. His only hope of being able to provide for his growing family relied on "The 'Silent Flute" seeing the day of light.

After rounds of deliberations and discussions for months, Silliphant and Bruce managed to come up with a script. Then James Coburn, Silliphant, and he pitched the script to The Warner Brothers. The production house was ready to back the script but only as long as the movie was shot in India. It was looking to use the money that its previous movies had made in India but which the Indian government was not allowing them to take out of the country. Bruce began planning the trip to India while Silliphant and Coburn were anxious.

The three flew to India, travelling the country length and breadth, looking for locations to shoot. Their search for location only went futile. They soon realised that filming in India was not a feasible idea. After having spent more than a month scouting for locations, Coburn and

Silliphant gave up the idea of shooting the film in India. But Bruce was reluctant to give up for unlike Coburn and Sillliphant who had well-established careers to go back to; Bruce had nothing. Tired of his stubbornness to make the idea work, James Coburn decided to back out from the project. With him out, the Warner Brothers were no more willing to back the movie.

On returning to the United States, both Siilliphant and Coburn offered him financial help, but an already hurt Bruce refused to their any help. Now the Lees were suffering from an acute financial crisis. The bills piled up one after another, staring at him in his face and mocking his inability to pay them. Now no other choice but Linda was having to find work to support the expenses and pay the bill. With no qualification and previous job experience, she could only manage to find for herself a minimum paying job.

Watching Linda leave for work hurt his alpha male sentiments, his patriarchal upbringing where it was a sin to live off on one's wife's earning. Bruce was a helpless man.

❏

The Tryst with Hollywood-II

After the failed attempt of kick-starting Bruce's career in the movies, Stirling Silliphant began looking for options in the television. Before leaving for India with Bruce and Coburn, Silliphant had begun working on a script for a TV series named "Longstreet." It was his plan B for launching Bruce, in case if the movie didn't come across. After Warner Brothers backed away from "The Silent Flute," Silliphant began writing a role for Bruce in "Longstreet."

The series is based on the life of an independent insurance investigator based in New Orleans, named Mike Longstreet. In his daily ordeals as an investigator, he takes help from his best friend Duke Paige, the chief auditor with Great Pacific Casualty. His life goes upside down when he finds himself a target of a bomb attack at his home, which permanently blinds him, and also kills his wife, Ingrid Longstreet. Recovering from an emotional and mental turmoil, Mike decides to live his life to the fullest as a blind man and to continue his work as an insurance investigator. His friend Duke continues to give him the insurance cases to solve. To help him with his cases, Mike hires assistance named Nikki Bell. She is initially hired as his Braille teacher but later goes on to become his insurance investigation associate. The other characters in the series are Mrs. Kingston, his mockingly exasperated housekeeper, and Pax, his white shepherd guide dog. As Mike tries to lead a normal life like before, he finds it hard to control his emotions, as he keeps revisiting the episode of the bombing and his wife's death. Bruce Lee had a reoccurring role in the series. He teaches Mike Longstreet the ways of protecting himself in hand-to-hand combats by applying Jeet Kune Do.

Before the shooting for "Longstreet" began, Bruce visited Hong Kong to arrange for his mother to come and live with him in the States. On arriving at the Hong Kong's airport, he was surprised at the welcome he received. No more than hundred people had gathered outside the airport to welcome his homecoming. It turned out that although the series Green Hornet, in which he played the role of Kato, got a lukewarm response in the United States, it was a runaway hit in Hong Kong where Kato, not the Green Hornet, was celebrated as the hero of the show. To add to his astonishment, in the crowd gathered to welcome him, were standing many television and newspaper reporters too. It was his first taste of stardom.

After soaking in completely to his newfound stardom, he made an offer of making a film with him to the biggest production house in Hong Kong, The Shaw Brothers. This legendary Chinese film production company was started in Shanghai in the 1920's by six intrepid brothers. It took shape as a major production house in British Hong Kong in 1958 after the construction of the largest privately-owned film studio in the world at the time. The Shaw Brothers went on to produce one thousand films over the next three decades, building up the largest Chinese film library ever. They produced movies in an assembly line manner, and most of its actors and technicians were overworked and underpaid. What made them the biggest production house in the whole of the Mandarin circuit (includes Hong Kong, China, Malaysia, Taiwan, and parts of Vietnam and Burma) was their distribution network. The owner of The Shaw Brothers, Run Run Shaw, was a middle-aged man. By the mid-1970s, his company was producing 40 movies every year, and around 250,000 people every day went to see them at 143 Shaw-owned theatres from Hong Kong to Jakarta, plus thousands more in Chinatowns around the world.

Bruce made Run Run Shaw an offer to do a film for the studios at a fee of $10,000. He also wanted to have complete freedom with making changes in the script and direction of action scenes. The offer didn't interest Shaw, which he turned down as soon as he came across it.

The biggest irony of Bruce's life was that his methods were too Chinese for Hollywood and too American for Hong Kong film industry. After being refused down being by Run Run Shaw, Bruce came back to States and began shooting for Longstreet. One of the most remarkable episodes of the show was the one where Bruce teaches the protagonist, Longstreet; Jeet Kune Do for the first time. It happens in the scene that Longstreet is requesting Bruce to teach him Jeet Kune Do.

"I want you to teach me what you did the other night," says Longstreet.

"I already told you, I can't," Bruce replies in a low voice.

"I'm willing to empty my cup to taste your tea," insists Longstreet.

"Open-mindedness is cool, but it doesn't change anything. I don't believe in Long Street's systems or methods. And without system and method, what's there to teach?"

"But you had to learn. You weren't born knowing how to take apart three men in a matter of seconds."

"True. But I found the cause of my ignorance."

"Then help me find mine," says Longstreet gazing into Bruce's eyes. After this, Bruce agrees to teach him the art.

The episode in which Longstreet trains in Jeet Kune Do, Bruce holds an airbag for him to kick.

"Kick me in the stomach as hard as you can," asks Bruce.

"Wait for a minute man, I don't want to hurt you," replies Longstreet.

"I'm holding an air shield. Come on."

"Ok," says Longstreet and then he kicks in the airbag as hard as he can.

A dissatisfied Bruce then teaches him the right way of kicking.

"Put your hands in here. Place them beside your sides," Bruce says punching in the airbag. "Now I want you to feel the difference when I put my body behind a kick," he continues. "When I count to three, EXHALE, strongly. I'll be kicking you." At this point enters Longstreet's partner, Duke. Bruce asks Duke to stand behind Longstreet. On the count of three, Bruce kicks the airbag, sending Longstreet flying in the air for meters. "Cool. I tell you that guy's fantastic," says an astonished and hurt Longstreet. At this point, Duke walks up to Bruce and asks him, "What is this thing you do?" To this Bruce replies, "In Cantonese, Jeet Kune Do, the way of the intercepting fist." He continues, "Come on touch me anywhere you can. You see, to reach me you must move to me. Your attack always gives me an opportunity to intercept you. In this case, I'm using my longest weapon by cycling against the nearest target, your kneecap. This can be compared to your left jab in boxing except it's much more damaging."

"I see… well speaking of a left jab," says Duke taking the boxing position. To this, Bruce throws a punch at Duke at lightning speed, stopping just before his face. He then says, "This time I intercept your emotional tension. I see your thought to your fist, how much time was lost." An excited Longstreet says, "and Lee's going to teach me all this." To this Bruce says, "I cannot teach you, but only help you to explore yourself."

In the episodes that were to follow, Bruce, not only teaches Longstreet Jeet Kune Do but also helps him realise the philosophy behind it. In another training session, Bruce teaches Longstreet the art of throwing powerful kicks. He moves swiftly on his feet, from one corner to another. "Now listen to the feet and listen to my movement. OK," he asks Longstreet. He then throws some kicks in the air, the sounds of which Longstreet listens carefully. "Relate to me. Listen to my movement. Now open your jaw a little bit. Feel the wind blowing? You hear the bird chirping? Now let it flow." At this command, Longstreet leaps in the air and throws a kick at Bruce. Bruce, impressed at his student's progress then asks him to kick once more, Longstreet asks for a minute to think. Bruce gets furious at this demand. "If you think then you still did not understand." "Why? I did it well, didn't I ?" asks a puzzled Longstreet. "You think a fight is one tool, one kick? You need to put a combination without thinking. And if you can't keep yourself from thinking, then hire a bodyguard or lead a less aggressive life. Don't charge blindly. Listen." Bruce continues, "Now you don't have the bird. If you don't hear the bird, then you cannot hear your opponent." He then starts moving with a light feet inside the room. He asks Longstreet to decide where he is. When he fails to find him, Bruce, pointing his fingers towards him, says, "Your thoughts are wrong."'

"I'm trying to learn how to fight, not how to think."

To this Bruce smiles and says, "May be well with you Mike."

In another scene, Bruce is trying to convince Longstreet to use moves like finger jabbing. He says, "Would he hesitate to gouge out your eyes?"

"But that's his problem."

"A bird, a cat would go without thinking."

"I'm not a bird, I'm not a cat, and I do think."

"Then that's your problem," Bruce replies.

In one of the most remarkable and philosophical scenes of the series, Bruce tries to make Longstreet abstain from relying too much on his intellect during a fight. He says, "If you try to remember you will lose. Empty your mind, be formless, shapeless, like water. Now you put water into a cup it becomes the cup. You put it into a teapot; it becomes the teapot. Now water can flow or creep or drip or crash. Be water, my friend." He continues, "Like everyone else you want to learn the way to win but never to accept the way to lose. To accept defeat, to learn to die is to be liberated from it. So when tomorrow comes, you must free your ambitious mind and learn the art of dying."

Longstreet was received well, both by the audience and the critics. Before Bruce could sink on to the felicitations coming from friends in States for his performance in Longstreet, he started receiving requests from radio channels in Hong Kong for interviews and conversations. Taking note of his rising status in the world of cinema,

Raymond Chow of Golden Harvest Studios offered him a two-movie deal at $15,000. Raymond Chow was an enemy of Run Run Shaw. Chow's offer was good enough for Bruce to accept without hesitation. In next one month, he started shooting for the movie. The sets of the movie were put up in a remote village in Bangkok. On his arrival in Bangkok, Bruce found himself in middle of a hot season, no mail service, polluted water, and to make it worse, no fresh food.

The film was to be called 'The Big Boss.' In the movie, Cheng (Bruce Lee) moves with his cousins to work at an ice factory after promising his mother not to be involved in fighting. When members of his family begin disappearing after meeting with the management of the factory, he breaks his vow and takes on the Big Boss. In his quest for vengeance, he breaks open a drug-trafficking ring, beating down wave after wave of opponents. The movie was to be directed by Wu Chai, but Wei Lo later replaced him, 'The Big Boss' was a breath of fresh air to the martial arts films and the Hong Kong film industry. It had a distinct storyline, crisp fighting scenes, and an engaging soundtrack. It showed a flawed hero in a modern day situation. The story (written by Wei Lo and Bruce) was very engaging and filled with suspense and action, and in a bold move for an action film, the protagonist remains almost sedentary during the first half as he must evade violence due to his oath.

The film was a huge success in the Mandarin circuit. It was released in the October of 1971. Overnight, Bruce Lee became a household name. It not only launched his career to a new height but also influenced his film-making style and the way future martial arts movies were to be made.

Although The Big Boss was made on a shoestring budget of less than $100,000, it raked in more than $HK 3 million within few weeks at the box office. In the meantime, the producers of Longstreet offered Bruce a new contract for the second season of the series where he was to be paid $1,000 for every episode. He asked his producers to double the offer, and they happily agreed.

Only a month after the release of 'The Big Boss', Bruce was back shooting for the second movie with the Golden Harvest Company. It was named 'The Fist of Fury', but was released in the United States under the name 'The Chinese Connection.' Chen (played by Bruce) returns to Shanghai, to his former school. He is taken by surprise when he learns that the beloved instructor of his former school has been murdered. While investigating the Huo Yuanjia's death, he discovers that an enemy

Japanese school is working as a drug smuggling ring. Later, he finds out that his teacher was poisoned on the orders of the Japanese School's master. He then sets off on the mission of taking revenge on his master's death. In the movie, Chen, using his master's teachings, takes on both the Chinese and the Japanese killers. The movie is a celebration of the Chinese patriotism against foreign oppressors. It was released in 1972 and was directed by Lo Wei. During the filming, Bruce and Lo Wei clashed many times on the sets over the creative choices of the film, and Bruce was frustrated by a lack of liberty and control in the filmmaking process. However, like the previous movie, Fist of Fury raked in millions for its producer. And this time, Bruce had managed to make his way into the hearts of the Chinese population all over the world. His portrayal of a Chinese martial artist who goes on to defeat one whole school of Japanese fighter single-handedly managed to hit the right chord in the hearts of the masses. He was now a national hero.

❑

The King of Hong Kong

Now Bruce was the darling of the media in Hong Kong. Soon his name began to be associated with every other diva in Hong Kong. His days started with addressing the crowd of reporters and fans gathered outside his house. It was now impossible for him to walk outside his house without a security cover. His feud with Lo Wei got much of the media's attention and in many cases was blown out of proportion.

He was the most sought-after actor in the country, with every producer lining up at his house to get him work in his movie. Many came with blank checks, many with promises of more than eighty percent share in the profit.

But none of this interested Bruce who had no intention of breaking his partnership with Raymond Chow. The two decided to form a new production house by the name "Concord Production." Bruce was made in-charge of the creative decisions of the company and Raymond Chow of the day-to-day business. Bruce wanted to be in complete control of all the departments involved in the movie making. From writing the scripts of his movies to directing them, he wanted to do it all by himself. Instead of charging a fee for his movies, he now demanded a hefty share in their profits.

His next was going to be called 'The Way of the Dragon.' He started working on its script. The movie was going to mark his debut in the world of direction. His decisions of charging a hefty amount for his movies and taking control of its production brought ripples in the underpaying and exploitive Hong Kong film industry. Now the other prominent artists and technicians started voicing their demands for better pay and work conditions.

The 1970s were turbulent times in western history. The collateral damages of the cold war had reached the countries in the mandarin circuit, the most affected of which was Vietnam. The war in Vietnam had drawn much contempt for the United States from different sections of societies. Bruce condemned the war on every platform he got. He wrote articles against it, and also mentioned it in the TV and Radio shows he was invited to. His objective, he said, was to sensationalise people against the slaughter-taking place on in Vietnam.

He declared he wanted to make movies that not only entertain his audience but also educate them. He wanted his movies to be both philosophical and entertaining at the same time.

During the filming of 'The Way of the Dragon', the term "King of Hong Kong" began to be associated with his name in the media.

Before starting to shoot for 'The Way of the Dragon', he awaited the call from Warner Brothers for a TV series named "The Warrior." But when the call did not come his way, he decided to go ahead with the shooting of the movie.

As mentioned in the previous chapters, among his pupils were the best Karate fighters of the country, Joe Lewis and Chuck Norris. In 'The Way of the Dragon', he asked Joe Lewis to play the role of a western martial artist whom he fights and kills at the end of the movie. Joe Lewis, unable to picture himself being beaten down by a short Chinese in the movie declined the offer. To this, Bruce offered the role to Chuck Norris who agreed to play the role.

In early 1972, Bruce began working on the movie. To make himself aware of all the aspects of filmmaking, he bought more than a dozen books on filmmaking. He was going to be involved in all the domains involved in filmmaking. Be it direction, scouting for locations, casting, choosing the wardrobe, choreographing the fight scenes, it was all going to be looked over by Bruce himself. And on the top of it, he was going to play the lead too. In this superhuman attempt of overlooking all these tasks, he had begun to lose weight very rapidly.

Once he started working on the script, the ideas were hard to come by. After spending days pondering over the plot, he decided to draw inspiration from his own life, from his time in the States, from his experience as a waiter, and from his leaving of Hong Kong.

He had zeroed in on Rome as the location. 'The Way of the Dragon' was going to be the first Chinese movie to be shot in Europe. The budget for the movie was set at $130,000. The movie was also the first Chinese movie filmed by a Japanese cameraman, Nashinoto Tadashi. Once the shooting began, Bruce turned out to be a demanding director. At times, he used to shoot more than sixty scenes in one day alone. But his main focus was on his fight with Chuck Norris, which was to be the climax scene of the movie. Most of his energy was directed towards choreographing the fight scenes on in the movie, which occupied more than a quarter of the script. Any unmotivated kick or punch meant a series of reshoots. Hui's task was made tough by the fact that most of the fighters, despite pulling out the fighting sequence convincingly, did not know how to react at the end of it.

Tang Lung/Dragon (played by Bruce) pays a visit to family members who own a restaurant in Italy. But gangsters want the land the restaurant is built upon annoying the owners, and forcing Dragon to protect his family as only he can. Things then intensify as the mafia sends more and more people and ultimately ends with a trio of highly trained martial artists coming to town to take out Tang Lung. Dragon, for the sake of his loved ones, must battle U.S. karate expert, Colt (Chuck Norris), in a Roman Coliseum.

Through the course of the shooting of the movie, Bruce relived many moments from his past and his experience on arriving in the USA. And unlike his previous movies, in The Way of the Dragon, Bruce highlights upon the comic side of situations. The movie, for most of the times, plays as a comedy, filled with comic sounds in the background. Although the use of weapons is a big no in the Kung Fu movies, Bruce, however, develops an acceptance among his audience for the use of "Nunchaku" through a spectacular display of it in the movie.

During the time of Japanese occupation of Okinawa about 350 years ago, attacking chieftains forbid the use of normal arms such as the gun, sword, and spear. So, the population of Okinawa turned to Karate and Kobudo, which is the skill of Karate weapons such as the Bo (a staff), Sai (a short sword with the two points at the grip), Kama (a sickle), and Surushin, a length of cord with weights attached to both ends for protection. Some Kobudo weapons were farm gears, which the clever farmers transformed into operative and protective devices. For instance, the portent of the nunchaku was a tool used to pound grain, which was later put to everyday use as a weapon. The nunchaku was built of two hardwood sticks, which that were firm-coupled by rope plaited from horses' tails. Today, the sticks are tied with rope or chain. For its simple exterior, it could easily be mistaken for a toy or an inoffensive bundle of sticks. In a combat state, though, it could be used to attack, block, smash, screw, and tweak.

Apart from Nunchaku, the movie has some insightful and philosophical dialogues where Bruce explains the subtleties of martial arts. In one such scene, when Dragon's Chinese hosts claim that Karate is better than Kung Fu, Dragon replies by saying, "As long as you're using your body to its fullest extent, to help yourself in the midst of violence to achieve one's goals, it's useful."

In one of the most important scenes in the movie, Bruce fights Karate champion Chuck Norris in one of the most formidable fight scenes of the century. In the scene, Bruce attacks aggressively in the beginning only to be blocked and attacked back successfully by Norris. At one point, it seems Brue simply can't break through his opponent's defences. A few kicks and blows and then comes the moment when he begins to adapt his fighting techniques to that of his opponent's violent and controlling style. But once again, he is made to touch the ground by one of the kicks. He then stands up and changes the game in his favour. He then traps and lures Norris to attack with a few feints, never really starting an attack. He instead dodges and weaves, almost feeling out him before gently giving some real attacks by way of ruses and counters altering from a violent fighter into more of a counter fighter working angles and wearing him down.

According to one of the newspaper reports of the time, Bruce predicted that the film would go on to earn more than 5 million dollars.

By now, the Lee family had moved into a two-storey house at 41 Cumberland Road in the Kowloon Tong area. The house had eleven rooms in it, enough for him to install a gymnasium and library in it. He also replaced his old Porsche with a new Mercedes 350 SL.

His name was misused by many producers and firms to garner some cheap publicity. Many in the newspapers claimed to have defeated him in fights earlier. Yip Man's son Yip Chun made one such claim. Such articles disheartened him a lot and made him furious to a very great extent.

He was everyday bombarded with invitations to attend different ceremonies and functions, but he rather chose to spend his time working on his next project. His next project was to be called 'Game of Death.' It was going to be a film featuring some of the best martial artists in the world. He had planned to involve his friends in the movie, giving them a platform to showcase their talent to a wider audience.

One such friend of his whom he intended to cast in the movie was the famous basketball giant Kareem Abdul Jabbar, better known by the name "Big Lew." He was one of his star pupils. The two started working out together in 1967.

After finishing shooting for 'The Way of the Dragon', Bruce decided to meet Jabbar who was in Hong Kong at the time. He narrated to him the idea of his new movie and asked him to feature in one of the roles. Jabbar instantly agreed. Although Bruce had no script in hand for 'The Game of Death', he somehow pictured a scene for Jabbar in his mind and decided to incorporate it in the movie at a later stage.

A few days later, Jabbar and Bruce commenced shooting the scene. In this scene, Bruce, a martial artist of every style, fights Jabbar, a martial artist of no style. After shooting the scene, he then went on a hunt for the best martial artists in the world of that time. The first on the list was Dan Inosanto who had mastered the ancient Filipino styles of Escrima, Kali, and Arnis. Bruce and Inosanto worked out for days the basis of the Escrima bout in the movie, which was titled 'The Temple of the Tiger.'

Through the 'Game of Death', he intended to denounce the reverence for martial art forms and illustrate that an artist needs to be better than his art. With no concrete script in his hand, he resorted to the traditional methods of filmmaking, improvising as he went along. Although there are disputes about what Bruce had in his mind for the script of the movie, a rough sketch of the storyline goes like this: Korean thugs kidnap Billy Lo's brother and sister, making him join an attack on an Asian temple housing a great treasure. The bosses of ever-increasing skill level protect the temple. Lo, and his band of martial artists must take on a company of Kung Fu martial artists, Karate black belts, a Praying Mantis master, a Filipino Kali master (played by Dan Inosanto), and eventually a seven-foot-tall black Kung Fu demon (played by Kareem Abdul-Jabbar). After beating them all, Billy Lo apparently makes off with the treasure (or returns it to its rightful owners? One cannot tell), defeats the crime lord who kidnapped his family and strolls off into the sunset.

Though he kept himself busy in his movies, his name never steered away from controversies. Many times he would find some of the other brands falsely using his name, some of the other movie claiming to star him, and some of the other person claiming to be his relative, friend, and even master. It happened once that his childhood friend Unicorn had asked for Bruce's advice and guidance for shooting one of the fight scenes in his movie. Bruce was generous enough to go on to choreograph that particular fight scene in his friend's movie. At the release of the movie, Bruce found his name and image all over the movie's poster. It claimed to star Bruce Lee and even went to the extent of using the footage of him choreographing in the movie. This incident left Bruce hurt and more sceptic in future.

'The Way of the Dragon' was a week away from its premiere in Hong Kong, and the tickets for the same were sold out minutes after they went on sale. The touts were placing their bets over how much the movie will go on to make. Meanwhile, the movie offers from every corner of the world were finding their way at Bruce's door. He was reportedly the highest paid actor in the world at that time. He had to turn down several offers, including the one from a Hungarian producer who offered him $2 million for two Kung Fu based movies.

It was also the time when then President of the United States, Richard Nixon, made a high-profile visit to China, the first after the rise of Communist party in China. The visit generated enough curiosity in the quest for the fabled lands of the east. Amid such excitement, the production house Warner Brothers saw an opportunity for a Kung Fu movie. Warner's president Ted Ashley called Bruce and Raymond Chow to the United States to finalise the deal. The movie was to be called 'Enter the Dragon.' After signing the deal, the first person to whom Bruce broke the news was Steve McQueen.

When everything in life seemed like a dream, he had the rendezvous with a nightmare. One day, when Bruce was shooting on the sets of 'Enter the Dragon', he received a phone call. On the other side of the phone was James Lee. He had developed an incurable lung cancer and was only months away from dying. On hearing the news, Bruce stood still for a while as he tried to gather strength to respond to James's words.

As anticipated, James did not live long enough to share Bruce's next big success. The Way of the Dragon released in Hong Kong, breaking all the previous records and went on to make $5.5 million in the first three weeks of its release.

❏

Enter the Dragon

Often called the greatest martial arts film of all time, in 2004, Enter the Dragon was chosen for preservation in the United States National Film Registry by the Library of Congress for being "historically, culturally, and aesthetically important." Apart from containing one of the best fighting sequences ever captured on screen, the film also boasts of a storyline, which robustly deals with the themes of decolonisation and colonial occupation. It is considered as the movie, which sparked the "Kung Fu Craze" both in the United States as well as in Europe.

Robert Clouse, who worked as a still photographer before directing films and TV shows, was asked to direct the movie. It is said that Bruce was highly impressed by a fighting scene in one of his movies and hence went on to recommend his name for the director of "Enter the Dragon." Because he was completely deaf, he hired assistant directors who could verify that actors had delivered their lines correctly.

The shooting for the movie began in the February of 1973. Ahna Capri was playing the lead lady in the movie. The other names included actors Jimmy Kelly and Bob Wall. Michael Allin wrote the screenplay.

In the movie, Bruce plays a martial artist based in Hong Kong. He is known for his great philosophical vision of martial arts as well as for his physical competence. He receives an invite from a man of mysterious nature, Mr. Han (played by Shih Kien), to contend in a martial arts competition taking place on his island. Apart from Bruce participating in the contest are Roper and Williams. The two were former army buddies since their days in Vietnam. They have their different reasons for entering the tournament. While Roper is on the run from the Mafia due to his gambling debts, Williams is escaping harassment by racist police officers and uses the tournament as a getaway. The tournament has the reputation of being deadly and extremely violent. Bruce, after entering the island finds out that Mr. Han, the organiser of the tournament runs a human and drug trafficking racket on the island. He is then approached by the British Intelligence Agency to go undercover and enter the competition to stop Mr. Han. Taking help of his friends Roper and Williams, he conducts a search on the island for evidence and clues against Han. This inevitably causes trouble with Han. In the final fight, Bruce uses a lesson he learned earlier in the film to defeat and kill Han just as the army reaches to end the bedlam.

Bruce's biggest concern with the movie was its acceptance in the Mandarin circuit. He had trouble accepting that his Chinese audience would not consider his character too westernised. Unlike his previous movies, which resonated the nationalist sentiments of the audience, this one was more inclined towards the philosophy behind the martial arts. He was seen by his audience as a country boy fighting for the rights of the oppressed workers of the factory. To Enter the Dragon, Bruce risked favouring the western elements at the expense of his generic audience.

The second biggest trouble he faced during the shooting was handling a mixed crew of Chinese and American actors. There was a shortage of translators on the set, which often resulted in confusion among the crew. The fact that there were no appropriate English words for some Chinese slangs and vice versa only aggravated the problem. To add to the woes, unlike in Hollywood where constructing a set was a matter of few days, thanks to the high machinery involved, such was not the case here in Hong Kong. Here, where labour came cheaper than the machinery, everything on the set had to be constructed by hands. This often resulted in wastage of time. Besides, there were reports of daily arguments between the director and Bruce over professional differences. The speculations that the project was inching closer to the shutdown were only made stronger by the long absence of Bruce from the sets. His unexplained absence fanned rumours in the newspapers and the magazines. Meanwhile, on the sets, real fights were breaking out among the different groups of stuntmen. Many of them belonged to different sects of Kung Fu and constantly sought opportunities to proclaim the supremacy of their sect over the rest.

Two weeks had passed, and there was no sign of Bruce's presence. It was Linda who came out with an explanation. Apparently, he was suffering from lack of confidence. A week later, thanks to Linda's constant persuasion and support, Bruce remerged on the sets. However, Bruce was undergoing intense mental pressure. He showed signs of depression. Nonetheless, the show had to go on, and it did. He continued shooting intense fighting scenes. Shooting these scenes, time and time again, sometimes 15 to 20 times, took a great toll on his body as he always complained of backache. Often he would get hurt while shooting such scenes. But never did he cut a shoot in between. Linda recalls that after returning home from the shoot, he would rush to the gym and work out late at night.

Bruce's spat with Clouse resurfaced in the media when he barred him from the sets during the shooting of the fight scenes. The two for the most of the time of the shoot shared a bitter relationship. Controversies on and offsets, intense training sessions and equally demanding shooting hours were taking a great toll on his physical and mental well-being.

Bruce had begun to show signs of a disruptive nature. Many times he was spotted talking to himself. His health deteriorated with every passing day as he was losing his body weight at an alarming rate. He began chewing cannabis to release him from his mental pressure. Months passed without him making any visit to the gym. He ceased to talk to friends and relatives.

As he finished shooting the movie, he assured himself that this was going to be his biggest movie ever and would shatter all the records worldwide.

❑

The Last Episode

The morning of May 10, 1973, Bruce was in the dubbing room of Golden Harvest, recording dialogues for 'Enter the Dragon'. It was like any other day in the recording studio. He rehearsed for a while before dubbing dialogues for different scenes in the film. After spending some time in the studio, he got up from his chair and rushed out. He manoeuvred his feet in the direction of the urinal. Inside, he splashed water on his face. He continued doing so until he lost his conscious and fell on the floor. Twenty minutes later, a colleague went to check up on him. To his surprise, he found him stooping on the floor. On being asked the reason for kneeling, he replied that he had dropped his contact lenses on the floor.

Back in the studio, he started breathing heavily. His body shivered and turned pale. His colleagues watched in horror as his situation deteriorated with every passing second. An ambulance was called immediately, and he was rushed to the Baptist Hospital. He had a high fever, was unconscious and responded to nothing. Raymond Chow and Linda were informed. Meanwhile, a team of three doctors under the supervision of Dr. Donald Langford ran several tests on him. A swelling was found in his brain. Doctors also found a small amount of cannabis in his stomach. Half an hour later he regained his consciousness. On being asked about the presence of cannabis in his stomach, he admitted to having chew a small amount of it hours ago. Dr. Langford strongly advised him against taking it. He told him if he started taking this again, it would kill him. For a second opinion about his health, he and Linda flew to UCLA (University of California, Los Angeles). There he was found clean. They found nothing wrong with him because there were no drugs in his system. Though he was constantly losing weight, he was declared 'fit' by the team at UCLA.

It was a troubled phase of his life. He was constantly losing his body weight, reaching a point where his body had only 1% fat. In 1972, his body weight was 146 lbs. When he arrived in HK in 1970, he was 155 lbs. In 1973, during the release of Enter the Dragon, he was about

135 lbs. By May, he was down to 126 lbs, alarmingly underweight. His relations with Raymond Chow were also becoming more and more bitter. He was also accused of having an affair with a Taiwanese actress named Betty Ting Pei. His growing isolation and deteriorating health, all pointed in one direction, the pressure of stardom. He had become a victim of fame.

Two months and ten days after his first collapse, on July 20, 1973, when Linda Lee received a call from Raymond Chow summoning her to reach Queen Elizabeth Hospital as soon as possible, she experienced what the French call-déjà vu. In the morning, Bruce left the house saying that he had an appointment with Raymond Chow at 14:00 hrs. They were going to discuss the script of the film "Game of Death." Raymond Chow and Bruce worked until 4 p.m. and then drove together to Betty Ting's apartment. Sometime later, Chow left to attend a dinner meeting. At 19:30 hrs. Bruce complained of a headache. Betty gave him a painkiller named Equagesic, containing both aspirin and a muscle relaxant. He went to bed after taking the pill. At 21:00 hrs. Raymond called Betty's apartment to ask for Bruce's whereabouts. To this, Betty replied that Bruce wasn't responding to her words and that she had tried every method possible to wake him up but only to no avail. On reaching her apartment a half an hour later, Chow called an ambulance and Bruce was rushed to the hospital. The doctors at the hospital declared him dead. There was no visible external injury; though, the doctors found that his brain had swollen significantly, from 1,400 to 1,575 grams. There were also bruises on his left temple, which appeared when Betty tried to jerk him off her bed.

An hour later, Raymond Chow and Linda Lee came out of the hospital to break the news of Bruce's demise to the journalists and fans who had swamped the road leading to the hospital. In the statement released to the press, the doctors ruled out his death as a "death by misadventure." In the autopsy, the only two substances found were the painkiller Equagesic and a small amount of cannabis. Raymond Chow later stated in the media that Bruce died due to hypersensitivity caused by the muscle relaxant in Equagesic. Many in the press ruled out Chow's explanation. Many began to speculate that cannabis overdose caused his death. Some went to the extent claiming that the spirits of dead Kung Fu masters took his life. Others began talking about the "curse" imbibed upon him by the underground Shaolin monks who were angry at their portrayal in his movies.

To put an end to the strange theories being cooked up in the press about her husband's death, Linda Lee addressed the journalists saying, "However, the investigation is not yet closed to the death of my husband, I wish the press and the people of Hong Kong would stop speculating over the cause of death of my husband. I don't have any suspicions then that Bruce has died naturally. I don't blame myself or anybody else for that matter for his death. Our destination is unpredictable. The only irrelevant thing here is that Bruce has died and he will never return. He lives on in our memories and through his films. Please remember Bruce because of his talent, his art, and the magic he gave us all. For those of you who knew him better, his words and thoughts will always be with us and will have an influence on us for the rest of our lives. I know, that the people of Hong Kong loved Bruce and are very proud of him because of what he has achieved, he had managed to get worldwide attention for Hong Kong. That's why I'm begging you to please leave him to rest in peace and do not disturb his soul. These are my personal feelings and wishes and that of my closest friends. I would appreciate it if you would listen to me and respect our wishes."

After a day of mourning in Hong Kong, where his family and friends paid their last homage to Bruce, his body was then flown to Seattle to be cremated.

Today Bruce Lee sleeps in peace, shielded by evergreen shrubs and a clear view of Lake Washington at the Lake View Cemetery in Seattle. The site is visited by more than 10,000 visitors every year. The headstone of his grave has a picture of his. Under the picture is written his name in English and Chinese, the dates of his life, and the words,

"Founder of Jeet Kune Do." Kept at the foot of the grave is an open black book. On the left of the book is a Yin and Yang symbol with Chinese writing, and on the right, it says "Your inspiration continues to guide us toward our liberation."

Bruce's death at the young age of 32 left many in shock and grief. His pioneering work in the world of Kung Fu movies continues to resonate in today's times. Since his demise, the industry has always felt a sense of void, as it continues its search of another Bruce whose work can be both admired in the West and revered in the East at the same time. Such was his charisma that since his death, the world had seen a number of martial arts movies, with new styles and new stars, but none has managed to equal the awe and veneration that his movies commanded. The world's search for the "Next Bruce Lee" continues.

❑

Famous Quotes of Bruce Lee

Quotes from the Pierre Berton Show (1971)

➢ Nowadays you don't go around on the street-kicking people, punching people—because if you do (makes a gun shape with hand), well that's it—I don't care how good you are.

➢ You know what I want to think of myself? As a human being. Because, I mean I don't want to be like as Confucius say, "But under the sky, under the heavens, there is but one family. It just so happens man that people are different."

➢ When you're talking about fighting, as it is, with no rules, well then, baby you should better train every part of your body!

> All types of knowledge, ultimately mean self-knowledge.

Quotes from his book 'Tao of Jeet Kune Do'

> I'm not in this world to live up to your expectations, and you're not in this world to live up to mine.

> Do not pray for an easy life, pray for the strength to endure a difficult one.

> Be like water making its way through cracks. Do not be assertive, but adjust to the object, and you shall find a way around or through it. If nothing within you stays rigid, outward things will disclose themselves.

> Empty your mind, be formless and shapeless, like water. If you put water into a cup, it becomes the cup. You put water into a bottle, and it becomes the bottle. You put it in a teapot; it becomes the teapot. Now, water can flow, or it can crash. Be water, my friend.

> Be happy, but never satisfied.

> Adapt what is useful, reject what is useless, and add what is specifically your own.

> Mistakes are always forgivable if one dares to admit them.

> A wise man can learn more from a foolish question than a fool can learn from a wise answer.

> If you always put limits on everything you do, physical or anything else, it will spread into your work and your

life. There are no limits. There are only plateaus, and you must not stay there, you must go beyond them.

> Love is like a friendship caught on fire. In the beginning a flame, very pretty, often hot and fierce, but still only light and flickering. As love grows older, our hearts mature, and our love becomes as coals, deep-burning and unquenchable.

> Don't fear failure. Not failure, but low aim, is the crime. In great attempts, it is glorious even to fail.

> I fear not the man who has practised 10,000 kicks once, but I fear the man who had practised one kick 10,000 times.

> If you spend too much time thinking about a thing, you'll never get it done.

> A goal is not always meant to be reached; it often serves simply as something to aim at.

> Knowing is not enough, we must apply. Willing is not enough; we must do.

> To hell with circumstances; I create opportunities.

> It is not a daily increase, but a daily decrease. Hack away at the inessentials.

> The key to immortality is first living a life worth remembering.

> If you don't want to slip up tomorrow, speak the truth today.

> Always be yourself, express yourself, have faith in yourself, do not go out and look for a successful personality and duplicate it.

> Use only that which works, and take it from any place you can find it.

> Forget about winning and losing; forget about pride and pain. Let your opponent graze your skin, and you smash into his flesh; let him smash into your flesh, and you fracture his bones; let him fracture your bones, and you take his life! Do not be concerned with escaping safely—lay your life before him!

> The great mistake is to anticipate the outcome of the engagement; you ought not to be thinking of whether it ends in victory or defeat. Let nature take its course, and your tools will strike at the right moment.

Quotes from the Movies

> Boards don't hit back (as "Mr. Lee" in *Enter the Dragon*: 1973; Bruce Lee's character said this to Oharra after he had broken a board in the air with his fist).

> A good martial artist does not become tense, but ready. Not thinking, yet not dreaming. Ready for whatever may come. When the opponent expands, I contract; and when he contracts, I expand. And when there is an opportunity, "I" do not hit, "it" hits all by itself (*Enter*

the Dragon: 1973; in a conversation with an older member of the temple).

> Don't think, feel. It is like a finger pointing the way to the moon. Do Nunchaku not concentrate on the finger or you will miss all that heavenly glory! (*Enter the Dragon*: 1973; In a training session with one of the temple students).

> A good fight should be like a small play but played seriously.

> Let him know. If I ever see him here again, he won't leave alive! (*Way of the Dragon*: 1972)

> I am telling you it is difficult to have a rehearsed routine to fit in with broken rhythm (*Game of Death*: 1978; during the fight when Bruce gains the upper hand).

> A few tricks from back home. You know I broke a promise. Never to fight again. (*The Big Boss*: 1971).

❑

Milton Keynes UK
Ingram Content Group UK Ltd.
UKHW011827151223
434437UK00007B/331